# EMIGRATE WITH CAUTION

## Nicola Butler

## Livingwords

A CIP catalogue record for this book is available from the British Library

ISBN  0 9535942 0 3

Published by Livingwords
PO Box 36
Dartmouth
TQ6 9YP

Printed and bound in Great Britain
by Antony Rowe Ltd. of  Wiltshire

JOHN...

The depth of our relationship will always far
outweigh any losses. Thank you for your unfailing
love and support.

# Acknowledgements

Without experiences and people entering our lives our character would never develop, so thank you to all the New Zealanders who have further enriched our lives. Especially to Sandy, my wonderful Kiwi friend, to Chris and Sally for their love and encouragement, Sheryl and Grant for bringing a bit of New Zealand to England – by living here temporarily – and many others who we still miss.

Judy Sporle and Sue Marston need a special mention for taking the time to read the manuscript, despite their already very busy lives, and giving me greatly appreciated advice and support.

My editor James Alexander was a pleasure to work with and has inspired me with a greater love of the English language. Trevor Peters Design agency came to my rescue at the eleventh hour, when a cover design change was necessary, and delighted me with their inspiration. As for my printer, Ian Lemon of Anthony Rowe has been so helpful, I can't speak highly enough of the service. Thank you also to The New Zealand Herald for their kind permission to quote from some of their articles.

Last, but by no means least are John and Alistair (my husband and son) the best travelling companions and friends anyone could have. If it wasn't for their patience, flexibility and support I would never have been able to write this. Alistair has been invaluable imparting technical knowledge and extricating me from dilemmas with my computer.

# PREFACE

Thinking of emigrating?
Think carefully!!
What are the real implications?

That decision to emigrate is so exciting, with thoughts of a totally different country and completely new start in so many ways. New home, new friends, new scenery, new culture...new smells, sounds and sights. Maybe you have been disillusioned with your own country or you are just thinking of retiring to somewhere with a better climate and lower cost of living – people emigrate for so many varied and personal reasons. Maybe it's just that spirit of adventure that led the pioneers of old to start again in a new country. Whatever your reason, one thing is sure: you expect it to be right, you anticipate happiness, possibly less stress and dream of the new way of life, a new home and so on. Will your dreams be realized, or are your expectations too high? Will the cultural differences be too great? Most people will have carefully weighed up everything (or at least think they have) before making that monumental decision.

This book is not aimed at putting you off emigrating. The hope is for those reading this to learn from our mistakes and gain valuable insight and knowledge so as to be aware of and avoid at least some of the pitfalls. This will enable you to emigrate stress free and stay stress free! The book is generated from our personal experiences of emigrating from England to New Zealand in December 1994 and living there for four years. It looks back over the time from conception of the thought to emigrate to the realization of the mistakes we made, and to our initial reactions on returning to England.

We lay out our thoughts, feelings, reactions to situations,

cultural differences, economical and financial implications, and experience of renting, building and the education system. It includes discussions we had with other migrants from Asia and USA, now living in New Zealand, and quotes from the National newspaper about the migrant situation. In short, it covers every detail the prospective migrant needs to know, including listings of useful contact telephone and fax numbers in New Zealand.

What is causing the long-term departures that made the net gain of migrants in 1997 only 450, when over 38,000, were granted residency? The grass seemed so green on the other side...what really went wrong?

If we can learn from our mistakes and experiences, we are enriched in our character and better able to enrich the lives of others. It is our actions rather than reactions that will determine the results.

# CONTENTS

# CHAPTER 1

## Initial thoughts and feasibility of emigrating

# CHAPTER 1

My husband John and I, along with our then 14-year-old son Alistair, lived in a private estate in Hampshire, England. Our three-storey town house was in a fairly prestigious and well sought-after area and very marketable. We had been thinking about moving for some time and looked around the New Forest and various quaint villages with thoughts of a cosy cottage away from the hustle and bustle of town. Increasingly, we found new properties had diminished in terms of room sizes and we really did not want to live on an 'estate'. Properties that looked wonderful in the estate agent's details, on closer investigation were situated right on top of a main road or had other detrimental eyesores in close proximity. At the same time, we were increasingly tired of the aggression and congestion, not only on the roads, but also in shopping centres and virtually anywhere you went. 'Sardine syndrome' was beginning to take hold.

How events exactly conspired I cannot remember. All I can honestly say is that one day John came out with the suggestion of living in New Zealand. This neither startled nor shook me. Indeed, many years ago, prior to our marriage, I had once thought about emigrating to New Zealand, so my reply was probably fairly nonchalant, as if he had asked an everyday question. We are both people who thrive on change and challenges.

As we discussed the possibility, anticipation and excitement rose. Having never visited New Zealand, initial thoughts were dominated by what we had heard and from reading magazines. Nelson clearly had the best climate and a number of people John knew, who had sailed around most parts of the world, including the famous yachtsman, record breaker and America's Cup winner, Peter Blake, said they would retire to Nelson. I personally favoured Otago, but this was purely from seeing photographs in magazines.

Well, the next step was to see if New Zealand would have us! Information from the Immigration Dept in London explained the points system and gave a guide for us to work out the feasibility of being accepted. Points were allocated for educational qualifications, work experience, age and so on. For the first time in his life, John's degree was of benefit, giving us maximum points for education.

We had decided by this time to visit New Zealand - we were not so adventurous as to go totally 'blind'. Once approved to emigrate, you have to visit within a year, at which time your passport is stamped as a returning resident and you have up to a year after that to take up that residency. Due to this, it made more sense to apply and know we were accepted prior to visiting. That way, our passports would be stamped at the time of our visit and we'd have up to a year to return and settle. The alternative would have meant spending a considerable amount on visiting, then applying, only to have to visit again within a year to make our final decision. Then we would have to take up residency within a year. Hope I didn't lose you in all that!

The paperwork really was not too daunting, so we decided to forego what appeared to be an extortionate charge for a consultant to do the application for us. Without going into the in and outs of the points and pool system, in the year we applied, the pass mark was 27. Committing ourselves to invest funds for a period of two years meant we could further increase our total of 26. An extra point was gained for every $100,000 (£37,000)

4

invested. Here lies our first error - so eager to ensure our acceptance we committed to invest $300,000, so giving us a further three points, well over what we required. The exchange rate at that point in time - November '93 - was 2.69. We were of course elated when we received that pale blue envelope with notification that our application was approved - only to be rapidly deflated on the realization that these funds had to be transferred immediately! We had foolishly assumed the investment would start as we took up residency, by which time various assets would have been released, enabling us to do that. The tragedy was that, being unable to transfer that amount immediately and bureaucracy being what it is, the Immigration Department were not prepared to simply alter the investment commitment to $100,000, which we could transfer immediately. Instead, we had to reapply with new medicals, application fee - the lot!

Our lesson learnt, we reapplied, committing only to invest $100,000. After all, we only needed one further point. Our application was provisionally accepted pending evidence of the transfer of funds. We duly presented the evidence and submitted our passports to be endorsed with the residence visa. The time period between actually applying and being accepted was approximately six months. This varies depending on time of year and the Immigration Department's workload.

During a conversation in April 1999, a Public Affairs Spokesman for New Zealand House informed me that the points system is slightly more flexible than it was in 1994. This enables them to lower or raise the points as necessary, in order to allow or disallow entry to coincide with New Zealand's requirements at any given time.

With the excitement of knowing we were accepted as immigrants, phase two was on the horizon and we organized our first visit to New Zealand. The master plan was to hire a six-berth camper-van (we like our space) and tour North and South Island over a three-week period, which included Christmas. We often went away at that time of year to avoid the cold British winters - another good reason for our emigrating. The alternative to a camper-van would have been to rent a car and stay in motels. This we personally felt would be more tiring, involving taking luggage and food supplies in and out of the vehicle. Also we could meet more Kiwis in the open air living, rather than being shut in a motel room. Travelling in a camper-van also has the added benefit of a fridge and cooker being constantly with you, making picnics altogether easier. It is also worth noting if travelling between Islands, that a rental car would have to be left in whichever Island it is hired. Taking luggage on the ferry as a foot passenger, then re-hiring and loading at the next port only causes inconvenience.

# HELPFUL HINTS!

1. New Zealand House address and telephone number at back of the book.
2. Photocopy all application forms and write answers on the photocopy, then transfer to originals. This prevents errors on the original and provides you with a copy to keep for reference.
3. Do not commit yourself to invest funds that are not immediately available to invest.
4. December can be windy and showery although still warm. February tends to be best month weather-wise
5. If cost allows, we would recommend using a large camper-van. For the three of us, plus luggage, the six- berth was just the right size.

# CHAPTER 2

# The 19 day reconnaissance of New Zealand

# CHAPTER 2

The reconnaissance route was via LA, where we had to change planes and were hustled through American customs by very officious and large customs officers. Understandably, security was a high concern and meant that some flights, including this one, had to identify luggage again prior to its re-loading.

How anyone can ever sleep on long flights I do not know. Videos appear to be shown just at the time one thinks it appropriate to sleep. Meals never align with one's appetite. Then there are those people who seems oblivious to the fact there is someone occupying the seat in front of them, as they slam the tray into its resting place or pound the seat with their legs in an attempt to make themselves more comfortable. We were the fortunate ones on this flight and had managed to obtain the emergency exit seats, so affording us greater legroom. It also gave us a bird's eye view of a rather interesting yet sad drama. The drinks trolley was nearby and despite the shorts being free, one lady - we couldn't decide if she was a kleptomaniac, an alcoholic or maybe even both - made frequent trips passing the trolley, at the same time surreptitiously taking bottles of whisky, brandy and so on and putting them in her pocket!

On arrival in New Zealand, our tiredness from the flight was transformed almost instantly to excitement, with the warm air greeting and embracing us the moment we set foot off the plane. We had decided to spend the night at a nearby Auckland hotel, so as to fully recuperate from the flight. This proved to be a very wise decision.

The next morning, we collected our pre-booked Maui campervan (the depot conveniently located close to the airport) and headed to a supermarket for supplies. To my astonishment, it was civilized - the people were not pushing and shoving. Kiwi fruit was incredibly cheap but terribly overripe, and as locals complained that all the best was exported, I thought it best not to verbalise any reply in case I was set upon as a culprit! Meat appeared to be a third of the UK price. Shopping was complicated by having to order in kilograms – after all, England had never really gone fully metric! Numerous bottles of water filled our trolley – we were not yet sure just how civilized it was here. Our caution with the water in fact proved wise and is explained further in chapter nine. Shopping completed and duly stowed, we were off – northwards first – to the Bay of Islands, a yachties' delight by all accounts. The intention was then to gradually work our way back down through the North Island, with a ferry crossing from Wellington, to Picton, in the South Island, booked for Christmas Eve.

We did not cover as much ground as intended on the first leg of our journey. The Bay of Islands was a good three and a half hour drive from Auckland and although we soon became used to the camper van, it was a new experience as were the roads. Our first Kiwi campsite was encountered when we stopped at Whangarei, two hours north of Auckland. What a difference to British campsites (in fairness last experienced in 1980) - here they are well planned with virtually every facility imaginable, even a trampoline which Alistair enjoyed greatly. This campsite was on a water frontage and we were astonished to find that trees were growing in the salt water!

Our eventual arrival in the Bay of Islands was enchanting. A quaint ferry at Opua took us over to Russell where we stayed for three days just relaxing and soaking up our first real taste of

New Zealand. The campsite located above the town, had a splendid view and was beautifully maintained, separated into tiered areas rather than everyone being huddled on top of each other. Soon this was not enough as we became quite territorial and resented anyone parking next to or within close proximity of us!

Patience never having been one of my virtues, coupled with the breath-taking beauty of the scenery we were surrounded by, I started to seek a decision from John on our possible immigration. We had really intended not to make any decision until we saw Nelson, which was high on our 'intended places to settle' list.

The scenery everywhere was beautiful, every journey was a sheer delight, with mountains such an aesthetically pleasing height and trees of incredible symmetry. There were wonderful picnic areas (well sign-posted prior to reaching them) enabling the tired motorist to relax in congenial surroundings. Some of these had picnic tables with trestle seats and even barbecue areas. There was an amazing clarity everywhere, which must surely be an artist's delight and resulted in our photographs being some of the best we have taken.

Wherever we went people were friendly, outgoing and warm: they actually greeted you when you went into a shop – something we became so used to that on our return to England, we automatically started to say hello in shops, but soon corrected ourselves... after all this was England and one didn't do that sort of thing! The most precious thing, sadly only two and a half years later waning, was that you could smile at a small child and they would automatically smile back! A smile is a spontaneous reaction, tragically lost in England as fear and mistrust has crept in.

We had planned a total of nineteen days in New Zealand and wanted to cover as much ground as we could to obtain a good 'feel' for the Country. Our initial impressions of the sheer beauty, space, cheap meat and vegetables, friendliness of the people, not to mention the joy of **not** seeing rubbish scattered by the roadsides (regrettably evident only two and a half years later) were all encouraging.

The fascinating history and culture started to be revealed at the museum in Russell: this after all had been where the first European settlement occurred, and later was the site of horrific battles as the Maori became frustrated at the breach of the agreement made. They had never agreed to be *ruled* by the Europeans. Even prominent New Zealand historians are in disagreement over aspects of what did or did not happen in relation to the Waitangi agreement, so I will not add to the debate.

Russell itself echoes peace and relaxation, a far cry from the bloody battles of past generations. The idyllic bays offer safe, sheltered moorings for yachts. A sandy shoreline edged with stylized coffee shops, an ice cream parlour and numerous well-maintained colonial homes. 'Cavalli House' (circa 1889) caught our attention, as we pondered on styling our future home on it. The equally old Police House, set almost on the shoreline and still operated as a police house, must surely be the most coveted placement in the police force! The shops were basic but served their purpose well. A touch of humour exuded from the local church, with its sign stating: 'Soul agents'. Could the Pastor have been an estate agent prior to conversion? Not realizing how quickly we would cover North Island and eager to see as much as we could, we left Russell after a luxurious stay of three days.

Driving back down to Auckland, our approach to Auckland City brought us over the Harbour Bridge. The expanse of high-rise buildings was framed with a myriad of sailing boats, row upon row, nestled in the marina. Auckland, city of sails!

We made a beeline for Queen Street (the main street) and were anxious not to spend too much time in this vast city with traffic reminiscent of what we had left in England: after all, one million of the 3.5 million population are in Auckland! Amazingly, we negotiated parking our six-berth camper van in the city within a short walk of the ASB BANK, a mystery to us today as we watch volumes of traffic fight for parking spaces. Our visit to the bank's specialist 'migrant banking division' was to be the sole reason for entering the comparative congestion of Auckland, and, with business completed, we were quick to depart.

Our tour took us fairly centrally down North Island with a one-night stop at Waingaro Hot Springs, in the Waikato region, north west of Hamilton. It has a magnificent campsite on three levels and we had the whole of the upper level to ourselves. As we enjoyed the relaxing, warm thermal springs, the strange smell of sulphur gradually diminished, as we became accustomed to it. These springs are reputed to be good for arthritis and are certainly relaxing for any aching muscles. Children are catered for with areas of fun including a water slide and in another area, a massive log stretched across the width of the swimming pool.

Our next stop was Lake Taupo, renowned for trout fishing, a sport we would start to 'tackle' - if you will pardon the pun! - on emigrating. The Lake is formed from a volcanic crater and measures 40km by 30km, which I'm sure excuses me for having called it the 'sea'! Motels line the edge of the Lake, which in reality could erupt again. It last shook the entire region 1,800 years ago. Taupo has the 'cleanest' feel of any of New Zealand's towns and boasts an excellent shopping centre as well as an active Arts program. It is a very convenient mid-way point to break a journey when travelling from one end of North Island to the other.

The camper van was a pleasure to drive. The added height gained from the front seats served to enhance the views and give a different perspective to that obtained lower in car seats. Certainly a six-berth was needed for the three of us and made it a lot more comfortable - not being 'happy campers' - we needed to make this as pleasurable as possible. Some of the narrower roads I personally found hair-raising but again we were impressed by the courtesy shown on New Zealand roads. We soon learnt to keep well over so as not to hold up faster drivers and this was always acknowledged with a friendly toot of the horn. The one anomaly we did find driving in New Zealand was giving way to the right. In certain situations, such as if we were taking a left turn off a road, any on-coming traffic turning right into that same turn-off had the right of way – a practice we still find at least bizarre and, in certain situations, highly dangerous. Hesitation is often caused, as one cannot assume that a person turning left will always give way, either through genuine ignorance or bad manners. Equally, we have seen instances of the vehicle behind the one giving way start to overtake!

A brief stay in Wanganui and a walk around the beautiful landscaped Virginia Lake gave me my first introduction to black swans. A pathway hugged the edge of the lake, with wooden seats at intervals blending into the foliage. A delicate white painted wooden bridge led to a splendid gazebo/bandstand over the lake, creating a beautiful focal point, leading one's imagination into a waltz and air full of Vivaldi. Back at the campsite, we had an intrepid visitor, a noble duck that braved the entrance step to our camper van, boldness born of inquisitiveness rather than hunger.

Carrying on down the North West Coast, we couldn't possibly drive past an air museum without stopping. Ohakea is a small RNZAF museum but still relays some of the aviation history of New Zealand. It is also actively used as an air base, affording residents and passers-by spectacular impromptu air displays as modern jets take to the skies on average once a week. A couple of miles down the road in Sanson, we found a delightful tea-room, the gardens providing a grandstand view of passing jets.

We had been advised to book the Inter Islander car ferry (from Wellington in the North Island to Picton in the South Island) as it would be full on the proposed Christmas Eve crossing. Having arrived at Wellington four days earlier than anticipated, we were delighted to be put on 'stand by' and after a fairly short wait, we were able to cross on an earlier ferry. Despite a mist and slight rain, the views as we cruised through the Marlborough Sounds were breathtaking, reminding us of sailing holidays in the Greek Islands. Numerous sheltered bays, bush-clad hills and houses only accessible by sea, a truly inspiring sight. This visual feast only became more delightful three hours later, as we disembarked from the Ferry and took the Queen Charlotte Drive scenic road to Nelson. This proved to be a very winding, narrow, tarmac patchwork of a road caused by potholes and erosion, somewhat nerve racking in the six-berth camper van and definitely not advisable to take at night-time! Wider stretches allowed for well thought-out picnic areas where we could pull off the road and relax, further enjoying the beauty that surrounded us. This location was even more enchanting as we heard the bell birds, an incredibly melodic bird song of two or three tones, that seemed to me to have different dialects in different areas! This had to far outweigh the beauty of anything we had seen to date.

A drive of an hour and a half took us to Nelson. With our anticipation mounting, we looked with different eyes, trying to absorb and analyse everything in our possible future homeland. Keeping on the main road as we headed for the Tahuna Beach holiday Park, we were thrilled as the road opened up to a curving bay framed by sand and trees right beside the road. Like all the others, the campsite was impressive and we duly claimed our spot. The Kiwis being great lovers of the outdoors, started to fill the campsite as the holiday season fast approached. Our next observation and joy was at how the children were so much part of the family – they were allowed to 'be' instead of the

British attitude of being seen and not heard.

To further assess Nelson, we took a scenic flight. When we went to book it, some members of the Nelson Aero club invited us into their bar for a drink and a young member showed Alistair all the planes and spent the evening playing pool with him. The hospitality really touched us. On returning the next day for our flight, we climbed into the Cessna ZK-TAH. The pilot having discovered Alistair's interest in flying, encouraged him to sit in the front and allowed him to briefly take the controls. The view was magnificent. As we headed towards the Sounds, it became more turbulent and the video camera leapt towards the roof of the plane. My stomach made a similar manoeuver and suddenly the flight was less pleasurable. Once out of the turbulence, the enjoyment returned. Regrettably, I pointed out what I thought was a dolphin in the sea below, causing the enthusiastic pilot to swoop into a nose-dive. From then on, I observed quietly, refraining from commenting on anything!

The long sandy beaches of both Tahuna and Rabbit Island, edged with fir trees, seemed to stretch for miles as we flew over them. The pilot's commentary on the area, discussing good places to build, live, go to college and so on, was all very helpful. By this time, we had started to look at land available to build on and to investigate costs, as we were now even more excited at the prospect of emigrating.

Leaving Nelson on Boxing Day, we went further north to Kaiteriteri. After negotiating steep winding roads, we descended into the midst of swarming holiday makers – a campsite to our left and an idyllic sheltered bay with golden sands on our right. In the interest of not adding to the over-population we decided to drive on through.

We progressed to the West Coast, only reaching Cape Foulwind, which was very appropriately named! It was a very bleak and rugged coastline, devoid of any endearing attributes. As a harsh sea hurled itself repeatedly at barren black cliffs, we decided to head back inland towards Christchurch. Kiwis with their origins in the West Coast have since told us that coastline does become very dramatic and picturesque.

Hamner Springs, notorious for bungy jumping, was our next port of call and I was mightily relieved when John and Alistair finally decided against doing a jump! We watched a young woman take ten minutes to actually jump. It all looked far too precarious and death-defying to me – just watching someone else jump was agonizing...and they do it for fun! As the cord reaches it's maximum length, instead of just swinging like a pendulum, the attached body is jolted back up against the rope as if trying to return to the platform from which it was launched. It then plummets down again only to recoil less violently before eventually dangling unceremoniously over the water. A waiting boat collects the body, who, if not dead from shock, is exuberant... surely only because the ordeal is over?

Somewhere between Nelson and Christchurch our minds were made up we would emigrate!

Christchurch is a lovely city bordered by the river Avon with the elegance of punts gliding tourists, lovers and the romantic at heart through over hanging willows, downstream to a land of their dreams. The river meandered through a park where weary office workers sought solace during their lunch break. A restaurant on one of the banks had incredible water fountains that resembled dandelions about to be blown. We found what we considered to be the best Air museum we have ever been to, with the exhibits set in dioramas and so sensibly run by exservicemen. These people have so much to share of their war and flight experiences and were delighted to talk about them. They were fascinating to listen to and it gave them a sense of self worth as well as employment. One particularly helpful gentleman, seeing our disappointment that there were no brochures about the museum exhibits, gave us a booklet, which he had written himself, cataloging all the planes in the museum.

The furthest southerly point we reached during our tour was Akaroa on Banks Peninsula, a town with a distinctly French ambience. Breathtaking scenery of massive hills and valleys led us along sweeping roads to Akaroa, unobtrusively nestled in a valley. The town had been descended upon by Kiwi youth about to celebrate the New Year and, needing our beauty sleep, we made a fairly hasty retreat back to Christchurch. At least another week would have been needed to comfortably see the rest of South Island. As we had decided we were going to emigrate, we knew we could explore the rest at our leisure when residents.

Having arrived in Auckland, we were departing from Christchurch and our final night before returning the camper van we cheated and stayed in a Motel – thoroughly enjoying the luxury of a bath and real bed. We discovered that even in Motels, the Kiwis really had worked things out well, with kitchen facilities and fridge enabling us to do our own catering. The room was excellent in quality and value, more comparable to a hotel than a motel as we know them. Rates were charged per room rather than per person and having two queen-size beds gave adequate room for the three of us. An added attraction was the indoor swimming pool, gym and restaurants. Since emigrating, we have always stayed at the same Motel when visiting Christchurch – it is conveniently situated only minutes from the city centre in one direction and the airport in the other direction. The cost was approx. $100 per room per night.

# HELPFUL HINTS!

1. Book a night at an Hotel close to your airport of arrival for one night so as recuperate from the flight before proceeding.
2. It is advisable to use bottled water, especially if frail or prone to gastrointestinal problems. (see chapter 9)
3. ASB BANK has a very helpful and efficient migrant banking division, address, telephone and fax numbers are at the back of the book.
4. Read the NZ Highway code: there are some differences one needs to be aware of.
5. There is a Fast ferry which takes an hour and a half, as well as the three hour ferry operating between North and South Island.
6. A Club class lounge (providing free coffee, biscuits and juice) is available on the slower ferry by booking at the Bursars' office.
7. List of Motels with fax and telephone numbers is at the back of the book.
8. Four weeks or more is really needed to cover the whole of New Zealand in comfort

# CHAPTER 3

## Decisions and preparation for emigrating

# CHAPTER 3

On returning to England after our nineteen day visit to New Zealand and having had our returning resident visas stamped, we now had up to a year to emigrate. With a business and home to sell, John thought the earliest we would arrive in New Zealand would be January '95. I made a positive statement (born from desire) that we would be there before the end of the year (1994).

Our journey back to Hampshire from the airport had us looking at a drab England. The countryside and towns were grey and bleak in the winter rain, with heavy clouds clothing everywhere. The land seemed flat and boring, ugly even. Buildings sat heavily on the land, all this further confirmed our decision. I was hit (not literally, fortunately) by the brick walls everywhere. Colours in our home seemed dark. The first two weeks after our return found us all feeling physically sick with the smell of the car fumes in the streets. We had never noticed this before, but the contrast between the clean air in New Zealand and the pollution of our hometown was phenomenal.

We would walk into a shop with a friendly hello, only to be looked at as if we had two heads. We suddenly felt as if we did not belong here any more and longed to be back in the warmth, beauty and friendliness of New Zealand.

The decision made, there was much to do. Quotes from shippers, complete listing of every item in our home to be shipped, photographs taken for insurance purposes, accommodation to be found in New Zealand, buyer for the house and company... the list goes on. We obtained quotes from three shippers, having ruled out some just by talking on the telephone – a few prudent questions as to how they would pack specific antiques had disqualified them and whittled down the yellow page listings.

We decided to consolidate our possessions – selling paintings and antiques that we were not desperately in love with and purchasing others. This was a thoroughly enjoyable process that took us on one of our favourite pursuits of visiting antique fairs and shops. Settees, we had re-covered – the clarity in New Zealand appeared to take a veil from our eyes, giving us a fresh appreciation for more vibrant coloured fabrics. The choice of these furnishings we believed would be more limited in New Zealand.

Our Mercedes was sold in favour of the latest Jeep Cherokee, and, by exporting the vehicle within six months of purchase, the dreaded VAT was not payable, but not having owned the vehicle for over two years, meant we would have to pay an import duty on entering New Zealand. On arrival, we found that the shipping cost was added to the value of the vehicle and then the duty calculated on the total! As the Jeep was not available in New Zealand at that time, we had felt this would be the better route to take. In retrospect (what a wonderful thing it is, if only it came sooner!) we should have taken our Mercedes – with no import duty payable and very saleable out there. The Jeep became available within a year of our being there – we are convinced the demand became so great due to people seeing ours, one of only two in the Country at that time: I'm sure we should have had some kind of commission!! We eventually sold ours, due amongst other reasons to the awkwardness of the short wheel-base, which made getting into the rear seats very uncomfortable as one humped oneself over the wheel arch.

The car market in New Zealand went from being one of the most expensive in the world to one of the cheapest within the four years we were there. This was a result of import tariffs being removed. Even at the time of our arrival, we had not been aware of the cheap Japanese imports that were available, which may have changed our decision to ship a vehicle from the UK.

The company, which after all was 'blue chip', sold far quicker than John had anticipated. The purchasers could not have been better to deal with and everyone concerned was very satisfied with the whole arrangement. The house was slightly slower in a declining market, eventually bought by a Scottish couple, who lived up to the reputation of their forefathers, even wanting written guarantees for electrical appliances in the property!

It was not an easy task securing rental accommodation 12,000 miles away. The only source of information we had (through NZ House in London) was a newspaper, for migrants, visitors to New Zealand and expatriates, called 'New Zealand Outlook'. This is a useful publication with information and advertising by various Kiwi Companies but it didn't contain any fax numbers of specific real estate agents. Through talking with the editor, I have since learnt that New Zealand Outlook would have obtained fax numbers for us and any other information we needed. Eventually we got in touch with a real estate company in Nelson when our future bank gave us the telephone number of one – we later faxed or phoned our requirements. We had set up a bank account with the ASB BANK at the time of transferring investment funds and were happy to continue dealing with them.

We initially needed a furnished property until the arrival of our container and were prepared to pay up to $250 per week (£104). This was high for Nelson and should therefore have secured a fairly good quality property. Eventually, we were told a suitable property was available and were pleased to have sorted it out prior to leaving England. It was great talking with these

Kiwis on the telephone – we enjoyed the accent and it kept our enthusiasm high as we dealt with more mundane procedures in England. Having booked a Hotel for our arrival in Nelson, most things seemed in hand.

We soon embarked upon a round of dinners and farewells and, as is often the case at times like this, one suddenly discovers that relationships had meant more to others than they had ever expressed. What fickle creatures we are, seldom expressing those feelings that in reality would mean so much for others to hear and realize.

The shippers descended as I departed for the hairdressers – one of my wiser moves! They were incredibly efficient and courteous, making one of the more unpleasant tasks less stressful. Our sole use, twenty foot container gradually filled throughout the day. We ended up with some over spill which they took away to wrap at their depot. This would have to go in a general use container and be sent separately. The shippers finally departed and we walked through our then very stark house, which was suddenly devoid of our personal imprint.

In case of time delays with our goods being packed, we had booked a hotel for our final night's stay in England, arranging a taxi for our very early departure to the airport the next morning.

There was never any questioning if we were doing the right thing; we were totally confident and excited about the future and starting life in a new Country.

From initial thoughts of emigrating to the actual departure, it had in reality taken two years of investigation and planning, an enjoyable but nevertheless tiring procedure. In view of this, we decided to spend two weeks relaxing in Fiji en route to our new homeland, a move to be highly recommended. Completely relaxing by the pool, one could let the stress of the previous few months drift away and start to prepare our winter white bodies for the New Zealand summer sun.

Fiji itself was clearly a fairly poor country. Travelling by bus from the Hotel to the capitol Nadi revealed small townships of grubby houses, with roofs of corrugated iron held in place by rocks, and poorly clad people along the wayside. Nadi appeared to be run by Indians and we discovered the population of Indians is far greater than Fijians. Taxi and bus drivers are 'persuaded' by shop proprietors to deliver the unsuspecting tourists to their shops, where once deposited, they are eagerly ushered in and encouraged to part with vast sums of money! All this was a far cry from the luxury and tranquility of the hotels. As I pondered on how the amiable, smiling Fijian staff at the hotels equated the opulence of these tourists to their own life-style, John helped my conscience by reminding me that the hotel provided income for them.

# HELPFUL HINTS!

1. Take photographs of all paintings and valuables being shipped, for insurance purposes.
2. List every single item being shipped.
3. If packing items yourself- detail everything in each box so they are easily located on arrival.
4. Going to the hairdressers or elsewhere if someone else can be around during shippers' packing is definitely to be recommended.
5. The import duty on cars was removed in 1998.
6. Try and find at least two clients who have been 'satisfied' with the service of your intended shipper.
7. We recommend a sole use container.
8. Do not try and book a flight for the same day the shippers are supposed to finish packing. Staying at a Hotel after shippers have finished will take away any possible stress that time delays could cause.
9. Break up the flight even if it's only for two days.
10. New Zealand Outlook telephone and fax numbers are in the back of the book. They also operate a visa and migration information line.

# CHAPTER 4

## The armour dulled – Organizing accommodation and initial arrival

# CHAPTER 4

We arrived at Auckland airport a healthy brown, clutching our passports which would now be officially stamped to state we were New Zealand residents. A change of plane would mean we could fly direct to Nelson. The excitement that rose in us as we made that descent to Nelson airfield was mixed with such a carefree feeling and no pressures – here we were without an ounce of anxiety, on December 28th, 1994 and despite it being 8pm, it was daylight and warm!

A taxi bus was needed to accommodate our entire luggage and I remember gazing everywhere en route to the hotel, mesmerized and in a state if unreality, peaceful and excited, yet strange. The hotel room, which passed my usual inspection, has even undergone extensive refurbishment since then.

Eager to notify the Estate agents of our arrival, I telephoned them and arranged to view the rental property the next morning. This was the first horror. The property we were taken to was in a very poor, grubby area and the tenant who had vacated the previous morning left a rather large hole in the sitting room wall! The house was squalid to say the least and we consider the real estate company foolish to have shown us such a property when they knew how much we would spend on rent. The absence of any social class structure does not mean an absence of predominantly poor or wealthier areas. This set back resulted in our spending several more nights in the hotel than originally intended, causing us to have increased costs.

Our armour of excitement and anticipation was so shiny, it automatically reflected this incident off without a thought. Only on looking back do we realize it was to be the first of many buffetings our armour would receive, to gradually dull it.

The one and only local newspaper had a column of rental properties and really would have been our best source. Renting as opposed to buying is a common practice in New Zealand, so properties are readily available. Via the paper, we found a lovely, small, well furnished and clean house, and we went to view it late evening when it was already dark. On being shown around the outside, which was barely visible in the dark, the owner gestured to the bottom end of the garden and announced that there were 'Natives' down there. This did rather alarm me and I couldn't think why Maoris should be in her garden. Was it something to do with land rights? It was a relief to discover 'Native's' to be the way they refereed to tree's common to New Zealand! Land rights?... well that's another story which increasingly raised it's head whilst we were in New Zealand! The other thing to watch out for is the 'Naked ladies' found throughout New Zealand...sorry to disappoint you, but they are flowers with no foliage!

On moving into the property, we needed some basics such as an iron, toaster, kettle and a television, although the latter I personally would have been happy to do without. The local electrical shop had a good selection, along with a salesman who not only resembled, but also behaved incredibly like Lenny Henry. We were stunned when the shop allowed us to take all the above items without paying and having no address or telephone number for us. How refreshing for good old trust to be still existing 12,000 miles away!

The house we were then renting only had a three-quarter width and rather short double bed. Our queen size bed would eventually arrive with the container, but as we also intended buying another queen-size bed (for the guestroom) we decided for the sake of a good comfortable sleep that we would buy it then. Having spinal problems, I found it essential to make sure the bed was comfortable. We were again amazed that the bedding shops encouraged us to buy a bed on the basis that if it were not comfortable they would change it! Although a wonderful idea from our point of view, it also raised the question of how many other people had also 'tried' this bed. Looked at from that perspective, we found it rather off putting. Three beds later, we were becoming rather embarrassed, so changed shops!

Before proceeding with the bed saga I must digress slightly. We discovered that many people, rather than stating their telephone number or name on answering the telephone, would simply say 'Are you there?' This was a source of great amusement to us and we would often respond by saying, 'Yes I am, are you?' or something on those lines.

Returning to the bed saga, we were persuaded by another dealer to take a king-size bed, in reality only six inches wider than the queen size, yet it seemed like a desert. The previous telephone answer took on a whole new meaning as we climbed into bed one evening and a voice was heard to cry in the dark, 'Are you there?' I should explain that the 'Are you there?' question originated from the early telephones, when the person one hoped to speak with often was not there!

The interim period prior to our container arriving had very much a holiday feel – our arrival at the beginning of summer enhanced this. With the delivery of our personal effects in New Zealand, we were dismayed to find the goods sent as 'over spill' had not been properly wrapped, resulting in damage and some of those items in fact missing. The main container however was totally intact. Sadly, our complaints over this were not dealt with in the same enthusiasm as the initial obtaining of our shipping contract. The jeep which arrived in a separate container had not had its battery disconnected, resulting in it being flat on arrival, giving us a lengthy, incredibly hot wait under the blazing sun at the clearance depot while a garage mechanic was sent for.

The arrival of our belongings meant we needed to rent an un-furnished property. Through the local paper, we again found a house that initially seemed ideal, as it even had a storage area for effects we did not want to unpack until settling into our per-manent home. Whilst lazing on the sun deck one day, I noticed a solid black line which, on closer investigation, proved to be a colony of ants on the move! We became aware that the house had a major ant infestation and duly contacted the pest control company. In fact, the pest control company was one couple with a fount of knowledge about spiders, ants, rats and such like. In the process of having our ants exterminated, I had a fas-cinating lesson about the ant, and discovered, for example, that the ants zigzagging their way around were actually the scouts. The outside of the property was sprayed, resulting in the ant in-vasion being redirected to the inside of the house. These were in turn sprayed and solid black patches of wall three feet wide and deep, told the grim tale of a slaughtered army! Probably in keeping with the ant problem, we increasingly realized the house was very grimy and spiritually did not have a good feel.

The decision to move was not taken lightly, having already emi-grated and this being the second property we had rented. Casu-ally looking through the rental section, we found a 'fresher' house with the bonus of a swimming pool, which enabled me to do some swimming teaching. It was a far superior house, al-though once we were installed, we found that paperwork in the office, as well as our clothes, became damp. A leaking water pipe necessitated the removal of the exterior weather-boarding to repair it and, once removed, we could see the back of the kitchen units. There was no insulation whatsoever! No wonder the house was damp and very cold. Much to my horror, a rat with a taste for plastic had caused the leak. Dining 'á la garage', it had a gourmet meal of part of the car engine, a bicycle drink bottle, and an endurance riding helmet. I'm not sure which was the main course! Newer properties do have stricter regulations regarding insulation. At that stage we had also not been aware of the importance of the sun being on a property and this house was in the shade all day and of course, this added to its coldness and dampness.

The ASB BANK, which had given us the name of a real estate agent prior to our arrival, proved to be one of the most efficient and courteous organizations that we dealt with in New Zealand. It leaves English banks still at the start line when it comes to customer relations and electronic banking systems. From the time of our initial contact and throughout the four years we banked with them, we were totally impressed. The only exception to this was an incident at a cocktail party in Auckland hosted by the bank at which their economist spoke and made a totally inappropriate joke, certainly not suitable for company with ladies present and even unnecessary in gentlemanly company. However, this lack of refinement and social graces is one of the downfalls of Kiwi society, as it would probably not even occur to them that their behavior or speech was offensive.

In their general banking practices, nothing was too much trouble. On telephoning one of several branches in Auckland City to obtain one Canadian $20 note and their not having it, they phoned around on my behalf to locate one. When I arrived at the branch to collect it, the assistant had kept me the newest looking note assuming it must be for a present! Talking to one of the International Banking Managers, I discovered that their staff have a two-month training program before coming into contact with customers and it certainly pays high dividends for them!

Living somewhere is very different to being on holiday and, once settled in our rental property, the 'serious living' started. Shopping centers were explored in more detail and, as we had anticipated, there was not a vast selection. No designer clothes shops, although some fairly good quality and certainly vastly cheaper clothes. This was not a problem to us because it was what we had expected and we were still thrilled with our new homeland. In everything, you get what you pay for and it wasn't long after being in Auckland, that the cheaper clothes I had purchased in Nelson suddenly appeared very drab and cheap by comparison to the better quality in Auckland.

Nelson has a way of life all of its own – unpretentious, casual, carefree and free of caring what anyone thinks, to the extent that anything goes! People tend to go there for the lifestyle and there tends to be a high percentage of 'New Age' travellers, people who have revolted against the nine-to-five rat-race – often from infancy! They swap their suburban home for a 'house bus', an incredible 'hippyish' work of art converted from a van into a mobile home, with a chimney and various added structures making it more resemble the shoe house from 'The old woman who lived in a shoe'. The bodywork is usually painted dark green or brown (environmentally friendly) and it sways and chugs along the road to its various destinations, defying all laws of stability!

The height of the holiday season from December to March witnessed an invasion of the weird and wonderful into Nelson. Parking in the main street suddenly becomes more difficult as the 'Centre of New Zealand' is descended upon. For some, all this adds colour and character to Nelson. A Saturday morning market monopolizes one of the three main car parks; smells and sights delight the senses and intermingle to create an air of relaxed excitement. Here one can purchase jewellery and trinkets hand made by the 'house bus' dwellers, organic vegetables, pottery, clothing, flowers and one can find all sorts of gift ideas.

# HELPFUL HINTS!

1. As rental accommodation is readily available, do not worry about trying to organize it prior to arrival.
2. We would recommend renting for at least two years prior to settling.
3. If renting, make a checklist of all requirements and take it with you when viewing properties.
4. An alternative to renting would be to buy an easily re-saleable property, before ploughing substantial funds into building.
5. Many of the properties have very steep driveways, so be aware that a container can only be unloaded at the property if surrounding land/driveway is flat and wide enough, even if unloading into a smaller furniture van, a sloping driveway will cause more problems.
6. Check doorways of rental properties are wide enough for your furniture to pass through.

# CHAPTER 5

## Education and boarding

# CHAPTER 5

The school years run very sensibly with the calendar year, the first term commencing at the beginning of February and third and final term of the year finishing around 19$^{th}$ December.

We had decided that Alistair would go to Nelson College for Boys and board. We did not know initially where we would build or even rent exactly, so it would be more practical. As an only son, we also felt the boarding environment would be tremendous fun for him and had visions of a nicely groomed young gentleman completing his education in this way.

The brochures of the impressive school building and boarding departments looked magnificent. We knew this was a state school but not knowing anyone in New Zealand and realizing there is not a social class structure there, we were under the mistaken impression that there were no private schools. This certainly looked on a par with the private schools he had attended in England. We were amazed and delighted to find the boarding fees considerably cheaper than his day fees in England.

During our reconnaissance tour we had looked at the three options regarding secondary education. Nelson College for Boys seemed to have the best reputation and it also had a related college for girls with some subjects being integrated. Nayland College, a co-ed school had an unfortunate and not necessarily accurate reputation for being for under achievers. Once living in Nelson, we met ex-pupils who we considered to be mature and well accomplished people. Waimea College (also co-ed) had a fairly good reputation. In retrospect, we believe that, for Alistair, one of the co-ed schools would have been the better choice. Unfortunately, this is one of those realizations that can only be born from experience or knowing people in the community that can give an informed and unbiased opinion. The ideal would be to allow a prospective pupil to spend a month at each establishment and let them decide where they are most comfortable.

Three days after arriving, we went to Nelson College to meet the Deputy Principal and be shown around. A jovial giant by all accounts, who, we were later to find out, had a tremendous rapport with all the boys and also later quite deservedly became Principal. He and his wife could not have been more welcoming. It was New Year's Eve and they invited us to join them for diner at their home. This, along with their company, was greatly enjoyed and appreciated.

Lord Rutherford, the great scientist, had himself attended the school and an impressive oil portrait of him hung in the entrance lobby. As we progressed on our tour, we eventually came to the boarding houses. Alistair was to be in 'Barnicoat' house. My light spirits suddenly sank as we entered a dark house and were shown basic, steel-enclosed shower cubicles in very cold, bare, concrete ablution blocks. I quickly held onto my smile as it tried to depart from my face and my countenance was eager to reflect my sunken spirits. The dormitories in no way resembled the perfect brochure – there were no carpets and they had an old, almost grubby feel. The 'lounge' area had a worn, torn piece of flat foam sponge (approx. 5' x 3' in dimensions) for students to relax on! I desperately held on to countenance, smile and spirits. Although horrified, I did not want to let Alistair see my feelings, at least not until I had talked privately with John. He was also unimpressed, but did not have quite such a mother's reaction as I had. Alistair was neutral; after all he had not been overjoyed at the idea of boarding. However, he did find an enthusiasm for it, which resulted in us dropping him off earlier than necessary on the first day. We arrived home and I promptly burst into tears with many mixed emotions about having embarked on that course for him. We were proud to hear later that he went over to one of his peers, held out his hand and introduced himself. Tragically, this resulted in a 'So what', as the boy marched off.

Boarding lasted six weeks – a traumatic time for Alistair who did not help matters by allowing reactionary behavior to erupt as he found himself in this alien world. In the New Zealand system, it appears that boarders are often those with problems at home and so they are sent to board – they are far from young gentlemen. The exception is those that live in remote farming areas and so necessity dictates that they board.

We later also discovered the existence of Christ's College, a private and by all accounts excellent boys' boarding school in Christchurch, to which the previous stated criteria regarding problems in the home does not apply.

Nelson College operated an 'accelerate' programme for boys of greater learning ability. Alistair was able to join this programme and ended up a year ahead of his peers. However, although not wanting to detract from his ability, I do feel the education system in New Zealand is not as high a standard as that of the UK. Maybe I should qualify that to read 'not as high as that of the private UK education system'.

Alistair continued to be taunted for being a Pom. He was physically struck on one occasion, and on another, his school bag filled with sawdust. Although he was no saint, especially when provoked, it was sad not to see a more welcoming nature for someone arriving from a different country. It was a far cry from wonderful Ditcham Park in England, where each child looked to others' needs and where, on his visit for an entrance exam, another child shared his lunch with Alistair.

Our perception of the college was totally wrong. Even locals considered it to be living off its good reputation of days gone by, and despite some excellent students, foul language and yobbish behavior was the norm. Sadly, a reflection of modern society and certainly not the College staff, who are as frustrated as most teachers these days! Even when collecting Alistair from college, I felt very intimidated by the boys' staring and aggression. On one occasion, a boy yelled out after the car at Alistair...he wasn't saying goodbye! Much to Alistair's embarrassment I stopped the car, got out and calmly asked the boy if he had a problem, he went very quiet and denied having said anything! That incident resulted in the same group of boys taunting Alistair more and telling him his mother was 'psycho'. As is usual with bullies, they won't face someone who stands up to them.

We were pleased that Alistair was going to jump ahead by a year, as it would mean he would not be in such direct contact with this particular group of boys, a fact that spurred him on as well. Finally Alistair left College a year early, having done reasonably well in his exams, to pursue his real passion of guitar playing. We could see no gain in him staying in that particular school environment. Some boys will excel no matter what the environment- Alistair was not one of those.

The educational qualifications in New Zealand are very different to that of the UK but there is a reciprocal agreement, with each country recognizing the other's qualifications. Universities and some further education establishments in the UK keep a list of NZ qualifications, showing their equivalent. However, the best place to contact is NARIC in Cheltenham. Sixth form certificate would appear to be closest to the UK 'O'level, taken in a range of subjects. The Bursary exam is needed for Kiwis to gain entry to Universities and in this is comparable to the UK

'A' levels.

The great 'OE' is often talked about – this is where students (or at least those who are able to afford to) take a year out to do their 'Overseas Experience'.

Prior to his seventeenth birthday, Alistair auditioned for a place at 'Excel' a Christian School of Performing Arts in Auckland at which he could major in guitar playing. Auditions were held throughout New Zealand, which included Nelson. The wait in the hall was nerve-racking, intently trying to strain a motherly ear towards the door he had been taken through. The room was set up with both video and audio recording equipment to enable his interviewers to review all candidates once back in Auckland. Other awaiting 'hopefuls' included another guitarist, a drummer, a singer and an actor. The actor, whether through nerves or sheer amusing lunacy – as is so often associated with great acting talents, gave us his excellent rendition of 'Frank Spencer'. In other circumstances this would have been greatly enjoyed, but with thoughts elsewhere it caused more of an irritation.

Two months later 'the envelope' arrived whilst Alistair was at college, and even a powerful electric lamp failed to reveal its contents, subjecting us to an excruciating days wait for Alistair. Before handing him the envelope we had a conversation aimed at preparing him, just in case of rejection. The few minutes he took to read the letter seemed like an eternity, then finally with a broad smile, he announced his acceptance. Elation filled the air in every direction!

The year that followed saw our seventeen-year-old son mature in a way so far unparalleled in his developing years. The majority of his fellow students were in their early twenties – he had tremendous University style fun with these new found friends. The course itself advanced his guitar playing skills greatly and developed song writing, sequencing and other related skills. His graduation day is one I will never forget. Alistair was one of the few to play his guitar on stage and I have never felt so overwhelmed and proud of him. John was 'incredibly' proud, leading me to think the overwhelming part is a mother's domain! The progression in his guitar playing amazed us, as did the relaxed confident manner and developing style. A smile between himself and the base player spoke volumes, drawing me into his joy. Usually I am cautious not to hug Al (as he likes to be called) in front of his friends but on this occasion I struggled in the knowledge I would find it difficult to contain myself. A mother's dilemma was resolved by her maturing son, who, on finding us at the end of the evening, straightaway hugged me – it was so precious!

# HELPFUL HINTS!

1. Be aware of the academic year starting at the beginning of February when planing dates of departure/ arrival.
2. Emigrating prior to or near to a child being 11 years old is often likely to make it easier for them to be accepted, with the school change at that age.
3. Thoroughly investigate all options of schooling. Lists of Schools at back of book.
4. If emigrating with children – especially teenagers – remember you chose to emigrate and your child has to go with you. They may need a lot of support through the changes.
5. Telephone number for National Academic Recognition Information Centre (NARIC) at the back of book.

# CHAPTER 6

## The Sun and Sea are North –
## finding land and legalities of purchase

# CHAPTER 6

Almost immediately after arrival in Nelson, we started looking for somewhere to build our dream home. No more moving – this would be it – sound familiar to anyone?

One really did not have the opportunity to build in England, and looking for the ideal location was exciting in itself. Only two days after arriving in Nelson, we had seen an advertisement in the local paper and arranged to view the land. It was a fabulous, three-quarter acre section and particularly appealed to us – with magnificent views of the Tasman Sea and hills to three sides, affording privacy and space. John found it especially difficult adjusting to the sea being in the North, it was most disconcerting. I on the other hand, seldom knew which way I was facing at the best of times and seemed to find my bearings more quickly!

The farmer and his wife who were selling the land explained how the plot was not sub-divisible. This was important with the increasing trend of people selling half their back garden for another property to be built on. Also he would see all the proposed house plans, approving only those that would be in keeping and which would maintain an up-market area. There was more land in the valley behind, where I could keep a horse, a childhood dream I was hoping to at last realize.

We had not expected to find the 'ideal spot' so quickly, so we still contacted most of the real estate agents and were shown various pieces of land and some houses, but none of these appealed to us. We went to look at a particular development at Ruby Bay, which we had seen on our reconnaissance tour. It was a good 45-minute drive from Nelson City and despite the dynamic views, appealing layout and quality of the development, after some deliberation we decided against it. Our decision was primarily based on the fact that we were looking for somewhere for life and should either of us become unable to drive or experience ill health in the future, it would be too far from facilities and civilization.

Generally, as we viewed various properties, we found the quality of houses left a lot to be desired. The British solid walls, giving soundproofing, were not part of construction here. One has to realize that houses are built with earthquakes in mind and so they have to be flexible. A lot of the houses are built on poles. This is to save cost on expensive foundations and also with a predominantly clay sub-soil, it enables building to take place on land that would not be stable enough for concrete foundations. The pole houses from our experience of renting tended to be so flexible that the whole house would shake when someone walked upstairs, an aeroplane passed over head, or a heavy truck went along the road – most disconcerting! There is little material between the main floor and the ground beneath, resulting in dampness. The ground under the pole houses tends to become an attractive area for mice and rats.

The room sizes in Kiwi house tended to be very small. We gradually came to realize that the reason for this was because Kiwis enjoy their outdoor living and would rather spend less on a home to be able to enjoy these outdoor pursuits. For the same reason, fixtures and fittings were generally very basic. The majority of roofs were coloured steel as the Kiwis (unlike us) actually like the sound of rain on the roof. I can only think this is due to their having so little rain, as opposed to the British deluges! Their priorities were different to those of the Englishman, whose home is his castle. After all, British weather is hardly conducive to such a continual outdoor way of life.

Having looked carefully at various houses for sale at prices up to $475,000 (£198,000), we realized that to have a home of the quality we wanted, we would have to build. We had looked carefully into prices of building prior to emigrating, being given square footage price indications, part of our initial plan had been to build our own home. However, now realizing the vast difference in construction, we can see why house building in New Zealand appears to be a reasonable price. Having said that, our home would basically follow the Kiwi construction with timber frames and gib board interior walls. In addition we would have an Oamaru stone exterior and double insulation between the skins, not to mention double-glazing, under-floor heating and of course, concrete foundations. The excellent weather in New Zealand does **not** negate the need for these facilities, as we discovered whilst renting!

We were increasingly drawn to the land in the advert and we had an architect view it to assess the feasibility of building there. Our friendly Deputy Principal and his wife also came and pointed out things we would never have thought of, such as where the sun rose, at what time and for how long it would be on the section in both winter and summer. These points we later learnt (after renting very cold houses which did not have the sun on them) were crucial. The majority of Kiwi houses did not have heating although some would have a log burner in one room. Our section passed with flying colours on all these points and was even virtually frost-free. We had the winter sun on the property by 9.30am and it stayed until it set, at which time the most amazing spectacle of dramatic red skies could be seen. In summer, the sun was on the property by 8am.

Having decided to purchase the land, we found a good legal firm: although we were encouraged that things were just done on a handshake there, a lawyer is essential. The land has to have a LIM or Land Information Memorandum done on it, basically similar to the UK Search. Land transfer deeds need to be prepared and exchanged. The sale agreement needs to be scrutinized, and our lawyer was exceptionally thorough and revealed a poor contract that needed to be re-written to protect us and other purchasers in that sub-division, in relation to a water company that one became part of. The town water was only supplied to tanks lower down the road and so a separate company, namely the title holders of the sections, was formed to maintain tanks and pumps which brought the water to tanks above the properties so it could then be pumped down to the houses. In essence, we were now Directors of a water company, albeit a small one!

Boundary marks had to be carefully checked prior to purchase. This was the responsibility of the purchaser and generally it really is a case of 'buyer beware'. Although an engineer's report was done when the farmer applied to sub divide his land, we considered it was prudent to have a more detailed engineer's report to make sure the predominantly clay sub soil was suitable to take the type of property we intended building.

We were told land purchase normally took a couple of weeks – ours took several months! The purchasers of the land below ours had in the meantime started building and had inadvertently cut a large chunk out of our land which had to be reinstated! Also, in the process of 'levelling' their land to provide a building platform, instead of making two stepped cuts, one deep cut was made. This had the advantage of their house being lower than our land, but necessitated the construction of a substantial retaining wall on their side of the boundary. This in essence was to prevent our land sliding onto them. The engineer specified such thick diameter retaining poles that they had to be specially cut, further delaying us from completing the purchase of the land. This was all very disheartening and we did continue looking for other land just in case there was something better, somewhere! Maybe if we had listened more carefully at that time to our inner questioning...? We even drove to North Island again, but we could not find anything so idyllic in setting.

A potential pitfall to be aware of when purchasing land is the 'paper road'. Tragically, some dear American friends of ours bought land in New Zealand without using a Lawyer. The house was well under construction when a neighbour objected as the house was built on a 'paper road'. These are roads that exist on paper only, in London. They were earmarked as possible future roads and many of them never come into existence. Our friends had to stop building immediately and lengthy negotiations then ensued. These lasted several months and at one point our friends returned totally disheartened to the States. The options that faced them at that point were to totally 'move' the house, which was already at an advanced stage of construction with concrete foundations, timber frames, walls and roof, or demolish it and start again! Suddenly, some agonizing months later and with no explanation, one of the 'powers that be' decided the road could after all be moved, to a position in front of the house. In reality, there is now the possibility of a road one day running immediately in front of their house. In practice, it is unlikely. How it will effect any future sale only time will tell, but inevitably a LIM will reveal it, providing of course a perspective purchaser uses a lawyer!

The predominant clay sub-soil can lead to slippage or 'subsidence', as we would call it. This is something to be aware of when buying land. A large development in Nelson had slipped and later been reinstated by the council but there was much local talk as to the actual reliability of that land. We personally felt concerned for people arriving from overseas who would be unaware of the background and possibly be buying into a problem. However, specifically asking engineers to check these aspects (and receiving a written report) should safeguard prospective purchasers.

There are beautiful locations and some excellent land (sections as they call it) available for sale in New Zealand. Sections vary greatly in size from approx. 700sq metres to several hectares and most have electricity and water to the sites. However, it is not unusual in rural areas to use water collection tanks, which can be topped up by tanker delivery if necessary, and cesspits for sewage. Very steep sections usually require a pole house to be built on them, but there are level sites available. It is worth placing an advertisement in the local paper for your land requirements as well as dealing with Real Estate Agents. Price is usually negotiable and we eventually paid $92,000 instead of the asking price of $100,000 for our three-quarter acre section.

When tackled with foresight, buying land and building should result in your dream home being completed problem free!

# HELPFUL HINTS!

1. Employ a good lawyer when purchasing land.
2. Try and enlist the help of a friendly local, who will have a wealth of knowledge about the area and any previous land use or problems.
3. Have a detailed engineer's report and ask specifically about any paper roads and land slippage.
4. Address, telephone and fax numbers of Nelsonian Lawyer are at the back of the book.
5. Winter and summer sun positions on the land and house are vital.

# CHAPTER 7

## The joys and traumas of building

# CHAPTER 7

Whilst waiting for our land purchase to go through, we had been formulating the design of our home. We obtained numerous ideas from interior design magazines and various houses we had seen over the years and liked the appearance of. These, alongside our own 'user friendly' concepts, we sketched on paper and we juggled with room layouts. It was most enjoyable and exciting formulating our ideas. We consulted a top architect who did the initial concept drawing at a vast charge of $12,000 (£5,000 with the by then 2.4 exchange rate). Due to a total misunderstanding, that charge would be additional to the working drawings, putting his costs way beyond us.

Hindsight is a wonderful thing and we now realize we could have bought ready-made designs and had them adapted at vastly less cost. The initial architect, as a result of our encounter, has actually revised the literature given to his clients so as to clarify costing. We ultimately took our concept drawings (really generated by us, but put on paper by a professional who charged us $12,000) to another architect who produced the working drawings for $6,000. However, like anything in this world, what you pay for is what you get and we have since seen working drawings produced by the first architect. These tend to be an average of twelve pages as opposed to our four pages. Obviously, from the builder's point of view, the more detailed drawings are preferable. I am sure it was only due to the skill and professionalism of our builder that he was able to proceed with the working drawings we had.

Having a strict budget, we went to a quantity surveyor to check that the house could be built within that budget. Where areas were looking more expensive we revised. For example, we chose a cheaper roof than we really had wanted saving $12,000 instantly. We cut back and reassessed at the same time, stressing to the quantity surveyor that we are perfectionists and would not compromise on finish and fittings. Finally it seemed we could go ahead and the house would cost approx. $320,000 (£133,000) although it might go to $350,000 (£145,000). In discussions with the builder, who had come by recommendation, we decided to employ him on a labor plus costs basis. He was also of the opinion that the house could be built within our limits and that his builders' trade discount would buy our materials at a more advantageous price. This at the same time would increase his discount level with the suppliers, as that increases with the volume of business he places with them.

The other way of proceeding would have been on a fixed quote basis. That would have entailed the builder undertaking to complete the house for a fixed amount and within a certain time frame. We felt, wrongly or rightly, that that could end up with things being rushed, and not the same attention to detail being observed. Also, if it did run over budget, with a small builder there would be nothing to stop them walking away from it, or going into liquidation. The majority of builders are one man bands employing subcontractors as needed.

Eventually, work started with the clearing of thick gorse and gum trees, which bordered the perimeter of the land on two of the boundaries. As this was done, the land previously obscured from sight began to grow before our eyes. At every stage we took photographs, giving us a wonderful record of the whole development and also enabling us later to show prospective purchasers just what was entailed. John meticulously keyed into the computer all expenditure, as we managed the account ourselves and all invoices were sent directly to us. This saved further costs as the builder did not have to become involved in paper work and payments. We obtained quotes from two glazing companies. The one which appeared to have the better product was given the contract. Despite their attentiveness prior to receiving the contract, the after-sales service badly let them down, so much so that our builder steered a subsequent contract away from them.

There was a small stream that ran through the land, and we decided to re-route it closer to the boundary, so giving us more useable land. The council had to be consulted and suggested – or rather insisted – the new stream should be rock lined to prevent erosion and guard against flash floods. Although there was seldom water actually flowing in the stream, it made an attractive feature when rock lined. One had to admire the skillful way in which the digger operator placed the rocks, manoeuvring cumbersome machinery as if it was an extension of his own arm.

The footings of the house were duly marked and then the land started to be cut into. Suddenly great scars appeared in a muddy mess and we frantically tried to visualize what the cuts related to. Over and over, we would stand in what we thought would be the lounge or kitchen. Unless prepared, it is quite a shock as the land is so drastically changed.

Weekends and evenings were spent 'clearing up' after the builders – this again helped save time and cost, enabling the builders to come in and get straight down to work. Increasingly as the house progressed, tea bags, cigarette stubs and remains of their food would be found on the concrete floor, something that we found disgusting and offensive. It may have been a building site to them, but to us it was our precious new home.

Before the house was completed we suddenly found ourselves having to make decisions about the location of power points and light fittings. Without the furniture in the house, it was not easy trying to think carefully where each would be needed. It helped to walk through the house and imagine I was vacuuming, so visualizing how far the electric lead would reach and subsequently where power points would be needed. Thinking carefully about all appliances such as electric blankets, hairdryers, computers and especially kitchen appliances and on which work-surface each was to be used, was vital. The end result was excellent, with more than adequate and appropriately placed points.

One of the best items we purchased was the Quantum water system. This is basically a fridge in reverse and not to be mistaken with 'solar systems'. Panels discretely placed on the roof would even draw heat from snow! The initial installation was expensive but would pay for itself in six years' time, and from then on, hot water would in effect cost no more than the price of running six light bulbs. The tank capacity was excellent and despite all three of us on occasions showering twice daily, if involved in sports or whatever, plus dishwasher and washing machine running, we never ran out of piping hot water.

Dealing with various trades people during this period was an eye opener in itself. Our cultural differences were beginning to show. In their friendliness the Kiwis automatically call you by your Christian name. In our 'Britishness' we found this over familiar and discourteous but tried at the same time to re-think our attitudes – after all, 'when in Rome...'

The British are great respecters of people's space and privacy, and this became an issue for us when tradesmen would arrive and start a job on our land without having told us of their arrival. The worst case was when I found a television engineer in the hallway of our home, after we had moved in. He had walked in through the back door, through the majority of the house, before startling me in the kitchen. I sent him out and asked him to go around to the front door, which was the door nearest to the room he needed to work in. I was horrified that he should have just walked in without knocking. He in turn really couldn't understand my attitude. The Kiwis are very laid back and the majority would probably be quite happy for a workman to go into their home, even during their absence from the property.

Newly made acquaintances would think nothing of entering your home and promptly stating, 'you don't mind if I have a look round' as they dive into different rooms before giving you a chance to reply! I for my part would always stop what I considered to be very rude behavior, by joking about it just not being the British way! Despite my 'when in Rome' belief, in a country that openly encourages immigration, I do consider that the native peoples should also have an understanding, consideration and respect of different cultures. I would never dream of looking around someone's home, even if invited to do so, I would be very reticent to. This does work the other way around and I believe equally that the British have been very negligent in their understanding and respect of migrants to the UK.

The house was nearing completion when a particularly high account arrived. We foolishly had not had a quote for this particular steelwork, accepting our builder's, 'it won't be very much' refrain. Only once before had I ever seen John go ashen. This bill tipped the scales and was the point when John realized the house was going beyond our budget. At that stage it really was too late to do anything other than complete it. Maybe we could have stopped and tried to sell it as it was to a builder?

Despite our doing much of the internal painting to save costs, as well as having managed the account ourselves and regularly cleared the decks for the builders to start each day, our $320,000-$350,000 estimate became in reality $503,000 (£209,000 excluding the land cost). This price was without completing ballustrading and floor coverings to the decking area, or plastering to some outside walls, which would now have to wait. It did include carpets, curtains, electrical appliances and all fixtures and fittings.

On careful analysis, we could clearly see that the quantity surveyor had been grossly in error on the man hours involved to complete the house. Prior to building commencing, we were told houses normally took about 20 weeks to build. Our house took just over 36 weeks to complete. John wrote to the quantity surveyor and a protracted written debate ensued. Questions were not directly answered and others twisted around. Ultimately, he refused to correspond and stated he would even charge us for his time in reading our letters. John subsequently contacted the quantity surveyors' professional institute and they were appalled by the lack of professionalism this member had shown. However, at the end of the day it appeared from talking to them, there was really no come-back unless we had the quantity surveyor supervise the work. This should have been made clear to anyone embarking on such a course but it had never at any stage even been suggested that a quantity surveyor be involved in any capacity other than costing.

Our lawyer felt to go to court, one had to prove a loss and it would be seen that we had an asset of $595,000 (including the land). The fact that we now had little finances to live on and would therefore have to sell the house was irrelevant. Two years later, we were still struggling to sell the house and had dropped the price to $485,000 with still had no sign of a buyer. Our antique dining table had been sold, as was the Jeep, to help us survive.

If building a house in New Zealand to re-sell, it is important to build to Kiwi taste. Our home was supposed to have remained ours forever but, as the necessity came to sell it and from talking with agents and Kiwis, one of the things we consider didn't help, was the European styling. Kiwis do not have formal dining areas as we did, or large rooms. They tend to like a property with open plan rooms sweeping into each other and, as mentioned earlier, do not spend much on their homes. In that respect, our home was over capitalized, with under-floor heating, double glazing and top quality fittings. It was these facts that led me to advertise overseas in 'Country Life'. Hoping the house would appeal to someone emigrating, I prepared a detailed portfolio with seventeen colour photographs and also a video.

The farmer and his wife whom we had bought the land from struggled to sell further sections, and we can only believe it was this that led them to allow properties that were far from 'up-market' being built. It is with sadness that I say that, as obviously the other houses built were also someone's dream home. However, for us to have built such a quality home and then have further properties of much less value built alongside was disheartening and of detriment to the value of our property. The only way around this (without some cast iron agreement as to types of property to be built) would be to hold onto the land and not build until all other sections are built on.

We moved into our home, which had suddenly become a burden, in the September. We were still hoping that we could both find part-time employment and resolve the situation.

Despite the liability our home had become, it was a truly beautiful location with a magnificent view and the house itself was what I call 'user friendly'. The exterior of white window and door frames set in cream Oamaru stone, with interesting angled roof lines, made a very distinctive looking home. The whole of the upper floor was dedicated to the master suite and had a balcony from the bedroom, a huge walk-in wardrobe, separate en-suite and a separate shower room. The main floor comprised of another two double bedrooms, an enormous, elegant bathroom, a large utility room and a designer kitchen and breakfast room with half-octagonal windows, opening onto decking with breathtaking views! The sitting room at the opposite end of the house to the kitchen also had half-octagonal windows and an equally fantastic view. The formal dining room accessed through double doors in the sitting room was more sheltered, set on the shady side of the house to protect antique furniture. The study of large proportions to house John's drawing table, our desks and computers also optimized the view. The basement level contained a two and a half car garage, a further room intended as a sauna and shower room, a cloakroom and an enormous storeroom.

It was a truly superb home, set in three-quarters of an acre of gardens that grew almost overnight with the amazing climate. Creating a garden from scratch on that size land was a daunting and tiring task. However, the rate everything grows did mean the garden looked good in a short space of time. Many people 'over plant' to give themselves an instant look garden, but really with the plants growth rate, I personally believe it is better to allow for the natural growth of the plant. This means plants will not have to be disturbed to thin out as they grow and will therefore flourish more rapidly.

# HELPFUL HINTS!

1. When using a Quantity surveyor, make sure he supervises the building work, so as to ensure you have come-back if costing runs over budget.
2. A fixed quote may be the best option.
3. When choosing a builder, visit properties he has built and talk with previous clients.
4. Buying and adapting existing house plans could save costs considerably.
5. If there is any possibility of selling at a later stage, make the house in Kiwi styling – flow-through rooms, good outdoor entertaining area, small rooms and basic fittings and fixtures.
6. Be aware that construction is different and one will not find the solid plaster walls as in England.
7. Be aware that invoices keep arriving for some months after completion and it is a lot more stressful to build than one expects it to be.
8. Contact number for Quantum water system is in back of book.

Views out over Auckland Harbour.

Auckland – Sky Tower, reflected in a high rise building.

The six-berth camper-van parked in congenial surroundings at Wanganui campsite.

A rare British style pub in Kiwi surroundings – what a combination!

The Inter-islander ferry leaving a typically grey Wellington in North Island.
Wellington is often referred to as 'The windy City'.

The magnificent Marlborough Sounds – viewed from the Queen Charlotte
Drive en route to Nelson, from the ferry terminal at Picton in the South Island.

Bungy jumping at Hamner Springs.

The enchanting River Avon in Christchurch.

Dramatic Nelson sunsets.

In contrast, only a two hour drive away, the Nelson Ski-fields – reached by this somewhat precarious road.

Building progresses with the erection of wooden frames, and the roof starts to go on.

Complete at last – a view from the rear of the property.

Fly fishing in typical scenic beauty of the New Zealand rivers.

The one that didn't get away, a four-pound Rainbow trout.

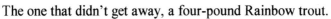

Jazz in the Park – Nelsons annual event for all the family.

Friends and family congregate in the Park.

# CHAPTER 8

## A different lifestyle

# CHAPTER 8

What had happened to the New Zealand of our scenic tour? The aesthetic beauty of the country was still there – opportunities that were not the norm in England were still there and one must be careful not to look with either rose coloured or cloudy spectacles.

Our first two years in Nelson were really concerned with finding land and then supervising of the building, making curtains and generally settling in. To be able to build a home and in a location like that would have been virtually impossible in the UK and certainly one of the attractions of emigrating.

Despite our own disappointing experience of house building (which certainly caused a serious dent in our armour), hopefully future immigrants will be more informed and aware of various procedures, such as having a quantity surveyor supervise the construction to safe guard themselves. Hopefully they will think more carefully and rent for at least two years in the area they intend to settle in. Where possible leaving options open and not drastically severing all links with their native home, maybe even not shipping out belongings for a year and leaving some finances in their country of origin. They should certainly obtain employment before finally putting down roots, whether part or full time. They must carefully assess the cultural differences and decide if these are things they can cope with, also carefully looking at the country's economy.

The climate in Nelson, so different to the rest of New Zealand due to its sheltered aspect, led to us being able to eat outside nearly all year round. Despite the crisp early mornings in winter, by lunchtime it was often 19 or 20 degrees Celsius. For the same reason as being able to relax in the garden, it was also important – especially in summer – to have any gardening completed by 8.30 a.m. The way of life was far more casual, particularly in Nelson. We never saw anyone wearing a tie, with the exception of attending a funeral and even then only a few would do so and most would wear their usual, casual clothes. We liked to continue to dress more formally and neatly, even our casual clothing appeared formal to Nelsonians. That more 'laid back' way of life is what many people emigrate for and having been there for four years, it may well be a shock once back in England. We have heard many tales of people being unsettled in New Zealand, returning to the UK only to return to New Zealand again! The grass is always greener on the other side no matter which side one is on!

Having settled into our new home we could at last start to relax more and indulge in pursuits that are not so readily available in the UK. Trout and salmon fishing are available to everyone in New Zealand, as opposed to the elite few in England. We all had 'casting' lessons and John and Alistair bought rods and all the equipment necessary to hunt for one of those intrepid trout! The word 'hunt' was the key, not the idyllic sitting by a riverbank, idling away a warm afternoon with a picnic and bottle of wine – yet another of our misconceptions! These trout were not willing participants in this sport of fishing, and who could blame them? Fly-fishing was the accurate and, to some, the more difficult way to fish for trout, the other method being spinning, usually used for salmon. This name difference really refers to the type of lure, a fly being a lure that 'impersonates' a real fly. It then becomes necessary to be aware of the hundred's of different flies to use and at what time of year, and which areas they are found in – these trout aren't silly! The spinner 'impersonates' small fish.

The hunt would commence by first discerning what time the fish would start rising to feed. This was all linked to water temperature, the weather and types of fly around. Clothing had to be of neutral colours so as not to scare the eagle-eyed fish. Polaroid sunglasses assisted in spotting the trout in the water, but I suspect the fish were also wearing Polaroids! Clothing, equipment, weather sorted, the 'hunt' would commence! The first time John went fishing was with a true enthusiast and it was only after that experience of travailing through rivers, over fields and rocks that John arrived home exhausted and newly informed of the 'hunt'. Was this really going to be a pleasurable pass time? As a family, we took the hunt at a more pleasurable pace – we had actually spotted some trout, but alas they must have also spotted us. Trout fishing is not a sport for those lacking in patience, and that, combined with the reality that a fish once caught, would meet its death by means of a hefty blow to the head with a rock, saw me take a back seat to the sport. My suggestion of a lethal injection instead, was met with raucous laughter!

The first catch will always be memorable to the three of us. John and Alistair had set off; I was going horse riding but first prayed (they needed all the help they could obtain) that they would both catch a trout. When they finally returned home, Alistair, who was elated and grinning from ear to ear, proudly produced a four-pound rainbow trout. I was thrilled but quietly asked God why only half my prayer had been answered? I decided that maybe on this occasion it made it more special for Alistair alone to have triumphed. All was revealed the following evening. It was our wedding anniversary and, as we entered the restaurant, I was greeted with a bouquet of roses from the owner and staff. How did they know it was our anniversary? I was highly suspicious and concerned that I was going to be serenaded or something equally embarrassing. After my usual lengthy deliberation over the menu, I chose a curry – apparently the expression on my face defied most descriptions when the waiter eventually served us with a large rainbow trout. I was bewildered, totally confused and it took a while for John's explanation to sink in, turning my confusion into sheer delight which still brings tears of joy to me. This wonderful husband of mine had actually caught a trout at the same time as Alistair, they both stopped off at this restaurant on their way home. John left his trout there for the restaurant to prepare and cook for us for the following evening. It must be the most romantic and meaningful wedding anniversary we've had. Restaurants in New Zealand are not allowed to sell trout, and they cannot be bought at all in the country, as the Government is keen to preserve the wildness of the fish.

Other trout were caught but usually put back. In reality we both preferred to eat salmon and they were more prolific in the rivers further south.

My childhood dream was at last fulfilled and I bought a horse. Horse management was very different in New Zealand. Due to the temperate climate, horses could be left out all year round taking care to use rugs to prevent skin cancer. This made horse ownership far less costly and accessible to the average person; paddocks were fairly easily obtained for approx. $10pw (£3.30). Riding establishments in Nelson were few and far between and left a lot to be desired, with poor fencing, nails sticking out and foreign objects in paddocks – it was a far cry from the precise riding clubs of England where horse management was taught as strictly as the lessons themselves.

We had three-quarters of an acre of land with our home and had made a small 'holding' pen which I used for a few days at a time when working my horse. I also had access to several acres in the valley behind where we had built our house. Having been an average rider at riding clubs in England, I very naively (but with assurance from the stud) bought a two-year-old Trakehner mare. She was 16hh, a magnificent animal with incredible paces and would obviously go far in dressage...but not with me! I learnt the hard way that one does not buy such a young, green horse without the experience of handling a young horse or someone on hand to assist. Being thrown off a few times was hard – one does not bounce quite so well as one gets older – but the day she turned around and booted me with both hind hooves on my right hip (causing a haematoma all the way down to my knee) our relationship deteriorated drastically! She was sold and is now doing well with an experienced handler/rider.

The right horse was just around the corner and despite the name of 'Rebel' he was a perfect gentleman. A wonderful 17.1hh Clydesdale cross who restored my confidence on and off the ground. He was only four years old when I bought him, but more experienced and with a sensible temperament. It became such a wonderful relationship that if I was grooming him and he wanted a drink of water, he would just nod his head over towards the water bucket and I would either lead him to it or bring the bucket to him. If leading him over difficult terrain on foot, he would indicate to me the easier path to take, using a nod of the head (after all, this wasn't Mr. Ed!) in the appropriate direction. Due to his enormous height and despite my being 5'7", mounting was made easier by his willingness to stand still by any fence, grass bank or literally any object I could stand on. He would lie flat out in the paddock with his head on my lap and was an amazingly responsive horse.

A less energetic and very enjoyable pass time was having coffee, usually at a table alongside the road in Nelson's main street, Trafalgar Street. Our favourite café/restaurant was where we had eaten the trout on our wedding anniversary. It had a good selection of light snacks and larger meals with an ever changing menu, friendly staff and a good atmosphere. The location towards the top end of Trafalgar Street also enabled us to hear some jazz on occasions when live bands played further up the street. In case you go there, it's called 'Pomeroys' and to us the only café worth going to in Nelson City.

Barbecues and informal eating/picnics with friends were always a pleasure; the Kiwis have a very sensible and automatic system of taking a plate of food or dessert to wherever they are invited to eat. It really helps lesson the load on the hostess and we gradually became accustomed to our guests arriving with some contribution towards the meal. 'Bring and share' meals were another informal dining with friends, where everyone contributed to a buffet-style get together.

Once a year about February, there is a Jazz festival, certainly not to be missed by any Jazz or music enthusiast. Various bands from around the country play at different venues throughout the city during a one – or two – week period, culminating in an all day 'Jazz in the Park' spectacular. People swarm onto the grounds from every direction carrying picnic hampers and 'chili' bins, the more experienced with seats and sunshades or procuring the best spots under trees. A lovely, carefree time from mid-afternoon to late evening is then spent listening to the Jazz and looking out for friends in the crowds.

The countryside is beautiful for walks (or 'tramping' as the Kiwis refer to the more arduous walks), mountain biking or indeed any outdoor pursuit. Swimming in local rivers is as natural to the Kiwis as walking down a country lane is to us. Only a one and a half hours drive away from Nelson are ski-fields but do not expect to find European facilities there, it is very basic and the road to it is somewhat precarious – as you will see in the photo section! Snow chains are supplied at the start of the road when conditions are particularly hazardous.

The continual outdoor way of life and sense of well being one has in such a sunny, warm climate has to be the biggest advantage over England. It is a relaxed carefree way of life not to be missed.

It was probably due to the increased outdoor pursuits, that we found injuries also increased. Owning a horse was not to be

Hazard-free; as a result of my horse walking into the back of my heel, I suffered a bursa sac injury, and concussion (with a subsequent three-day stay in hospital) from dismounting head, instead of feet first! A harmless walk in the countryside revealed an end of rusty wire fencing sticking out of the ground, but only after it had penetrated my shoe and foot, necessitating a tetanus injection. These incidents and various ailments in the family enabled us to test the health system. We had taken out private health care with Southern Cross, whom we were very impressed by as they always paid claims promptly.

In general, each visit to a GP has to be paid for and on average costs $36 (£12). If referred to a specialist in the hospital system by your GP, there is no charge for the consultation with the specialist. However, as in the UK, one can choose to see a specialist privately. The state health hospitalization system, which I experienced due to my concussion, was excellent. Specialists, both in the state and private health care systems showed equal care and knowledge.

We tended to find that our insurance premiums balanced with our claims, but of course there can always be something unexpected, so we personally consider health insurance important. On certain procedures, Southern Cross have to give prior approval, but this was always easily obtained over the telephone and confirmed in writing. Like UK private health schemes, each company offers various levels of cover and like the UK companies, premiums are constantly being increased!

Finding a good dentist was hard work. The majority of Kiwis we spoke to have not been to a dentist for a number of years. With all dentistry having to be paid for, sadly it was neglected by a high percentage of the population. When we told people of the system in the UK of going every four months and seeing a hygienist, they were amazed. A standard incisor white filling would cost on average $50(£16.60), a molar up to $120 (£40), and a root canal filling can cost up to $1400(£467). We did not come across any scheme such as 'Denplan' although certain levels of cover within the medical insurance allow a sum for dentistry.

# HELPFUL HINTS!

1. A fishing license has to be applied for in different regions but is only the equivalent of £15 for a year!
2. Be prepared for a totally casual way of life and recognize you may yearn for more formality at times.
3. Medical Insurance can be arranged prior to arrival, to start from date of arrival. Southern Cross telephone and fax numbers are in the back of the book.

# CHAPTER 9

## The naked truth –
## Culture and economy uncovered

# CHAPTER 9

On arriving in Nelson, we had discovered that many of the people we talked with had more than one job. Our initial thoughts about that were that they were incredibly industrious people. We later discovered the stark reality is that wages are incredibly low, the average hourly rate was $10, (£3.30 which was declared the minimum wage in the UK in 1999). A student in a supermarket would earn just $5 an hour, £1.60! The leading retailer appears to be 'The Warehouse', literally a warehouse-type store, selling a vast range of budget priced goods. We rapidly discovered there were minimal retailers in any field selling true quality products. People went for budget prices simply because their wages are so low, creating a perpetuating poverty spirit.

Supermarkets were a far cry from Marks and Spencer (or the Marks and Spencer we knew prior to emigrating!). The health and safety standards left a lot to be desired. Boxes containing foods were placed on the floor while the shelves were filled: rotting food was left on display for a month in one case, despite having pointed it out to a Manager! Checkout operators would think nothing of placing carrier bags of food on the floor, wrapping produce in newspaper or placing washing detergents in a bag with food products. The worst horror was seeing a cockroach scurry along a counter where spilled coffee beans had been accumulating. During 1998, some more up-market food chains opened in Nelson and with them a higher standard of display and cleanliness (on the surface at least!). These latest chains were already operating in the North Island and we had experienced them whilst touring. Again, it's not until you start to live somewhere that you really pay attention to these details.

The water supply in Nelson, from the layman's perspective, is recognized as being of very poor quality, frequently having a yellow appearance. Water comes from the reservoirs and at times of heavy rainfall, the muddy water washes from the hillsides and contaminates the water supply. A particular bug called giardia can be found in contaminated water. The bug, which can cause severe diarrhoea, is very difficult to get rid of and has entered the rivers due to people urinating and defecating on the land. There was more than one occasion, whilst living in Nelson, that residents were advised to boil water for at least three minutes – the time taken to destroy the giardia bug. Only when our house was built, and we had a water filter fitted to the drinking water supply, did we feel happier about drinking tap water, having bought bottled water up until that time.

Having consulted the Chairman of a Water Company in New Zealand, the above commonly held perspective needs to be clarified for total accuracy. It appears in days gone by that drinking water did not need treating and could be taken and drunk directly from rivers, lakes and dams. It was the growth in the numbers of people and livestock resulting in application of farm chemicals, aerial top-dressing, not to mention the urinating and so on, that necessitated the addition of chemicals (predominantly chlorine) to the water to maintain it's quality. As people and animals continue to increase with all the knock-on effects, higher standards of drinking water treatment are needed and have in fact been mandated. Anglian Water Company is a leader in this field.

Cultural differences are inevitable and, having lived in Africa, working with Africans and Americans, as well as having traveled extensively, one respects other cultures and the idiosyncrasies of each culture – including our own! Let's face it, to many, the British are aloof and pompous, with a class structure that fascinates some and appals others. Equally, they are recognized for their humour and preciseness, quaint afternoon teas and etiquette. Every culture is different and individual cultures should be treasured – they are an integral part of one's make up. I almost think there is a 'gene' for culture! I for one am proud of being British and have probably realized for the first time just how deep that culture is. Once British always British!

Once African always African also applies. Whatever an individual's culture, it cannot and should not be changed, it is a vital part of one's make up. This has so impressed upon me that I now believe children orphaned in countries throughout the world should, wherever possible, be cared for in the country of their birth. The organization Hope and Homes for Children have obviously grasped how crucial this is, as they establish orphanages in war-torn countries. So many well-meaning people think it preferable to take the children out of their birth country (I would have been amongst that misguided group) but this will undoubtedly cause identity problems at some point in their lives.

We had a misconception that Kiwis were culturally very similar to us, although we found them to be more outgoing and friendly than the average British person. Being outgoing people ourselves, this was something we enjoyed. However, the outgoing nature steps beyond the bounds of decency when it neglects confidentiality, privacy and respect. It soon became apparent that everybody seemed to know everybody else's business. People would openly relate how many times Mr. Bloggs had been married or what his financial problems were – something that shocked us time and again. It also resulted in us being very cautious as to what we said to anyone.

John particularly missed the British newspapers. With the exception of the Auckland produced 'New Zealand Herald', papers published very little (if anything) of worldwide news. It was incredibly difficult for South Island inhabitants to obtain 'The Herald', unless one took out a subscription with them directly from Auckland, so receiving the paper by post two days late.

Television was not of the same high quality as the BBC. We decided that it went deeper than the lack of quality, it was a guide in itself as to a country's culture. The majority of advertising was so amateurish and cringingly ham, not to mention earthy and course! Even major companies advertising there reflected this earthiness. For example, Caltex petrol, depicted a urinating baby in an advertisement – something the Kiwis find hilarious. In reality, any company needs to adapt its advertising to reach their chosen market and therefore needs a good knowledge of cultural differences worldwide. Owner/operators would often do their own walk-on ads, maybe fulfilling some life long desire to be an actor? It appealed to the average Kiwi. Basically there was a total lack of sophistication and refinement, from a British perspective of course.

The same lack of professionalism, sophistication and refinement prevailed when dealing with small businesses. This was particularly prevalent in Nelson and it must be noted that Auckland is very different. One particularly infuriating trait is the inability to apologize. An apology can be made without admitting liability and greatly deflate a situation. On one occasion, our glazier returned with fly screens, which had been made the wrong size, already months overdue. Still wrong, we were told he would be back the next day – ten days later he arrived. As no apology was immediately forthcoming, I tried to steer one out of him, with lighthearted comments like: 'What happened? You said you'd be back the next day.' Instead of a polite: ' Oh I'm sorry – we had a problem', The reply was an irritated, 'Well, I'm not perfect...' He drastically missed his opportunity, so I was more direct: 'Well, an apology would be more helpful!'

This leads us onto the next deep frustration we experienced. The majority of Kiwi men (again more prevalent in Nelson) have a problem when dealing with ladies. In fact, more accurately, they think they should only deal with men. John and I own and deal with everything equally and he was tremendous in supporting me in the rather archaic and frustrating situation we, or rather I, found myself in. In discussions in shops, car dealers, building merchants and so on, salesmen would even avoid eye contact with me and direct all comments to John. As a true gentleman, John would tell them I was dealing with that particular issue so they would have to ask me! We would receive a telephone call regarding our property and the man on the line would ask to speak to my husband. I would, of course, ask what it was in connection with, and when told, I would say, 'Well you can speak to me.' One situation was so extreme that someone still insisted on speaking to John, so I told him if he were not prepared to speak to me he could not deal with us. Over the four years, my fighting spirit over that sort of attitude probably subsided slightly, although the frustration was often still there.

Restaurants too came under British scrutiny and left many a waitress bemused by our insistence that they did not start to clear plates from our table when one of our party was still eating! I have since discovered this also happens in Canada and they actually consider it ill-mannered to leave unclean plates at the table.

Generally, peoples table manners left a lot to be desired. With few exceptions, we found people did not hold knives and forks correctly, would wave them around whilst eating and be most unrefined in their actual eating. Lack of refinement and culture existed in many areas! There must be a percentage of immigrants who see the shortcomings and balance it all against the wonderful climate, aesthetic beauty and more casual way of life. Also there would undoubtedly be a percentage that would not even notice the lack of refinement.

Kiwi ladies seemed forever baking some delicacy. This proved to be necessary due to the fact that for some inexplicable reason, succulent, fluffy gateaux and cakes were not available in the shops. No Marks and Spencer trifles, apple turnovers or fresh cream sponges, let alone cream assortments there! Bakers did exist but apart from some wonderful savories, they sold what we considered stodgy or saw-dusty cakes, so home baking was essential! Auckland was a whole new refreshing world after our time in Nelson, with more traditional patisseries.

We soon discovered a new language existed for various everyday objects. 'Togs' was a less cumbersome word that gradually grew on us for 'Swimming costume/trunks'. The most confusing was the use of 'chips' for crisps, meaning that french fries became 'hot chips'. Sweets of every description became 'lollies', so the iced lolly that we know became 'ice block'.

Within the period we were in New Zealand we saw Nabisco, the biscuit manufacturer, withdraw back to Australia, the Honda depot close and clothing manufacturers close. Increasingly, there were no large companies to provide work. As New Zealand removed import duties from goods coming into the country, they further killed their own industries. A factory closure involving 200 employees may not sound vast to England with its 67 million plus population. However, with New Zealand's population of only 3.5 million, its impact on the community was far greater and it was heart-breaking to see women in tears as factories closed.

As a family, one day we debated what New Zealand had to offer the world and how its economy could be improved. Our conclusions were that the wine industry was probably one of its better assets. Tourism was not going to be the answer. Yes aesthetically it is a beautiful country and operators such as Maui and various motels/hotels may be able to survive and even show good profits – at least until the Asian crisis hit! We mused on how it could export tourism – visual reality?

New Zealand needed to be able to create jobs and wealth – it doesn't have the IBMs. It's own car industry was destroyed by cheap Japanese imports. We could only see the economy getting worse and worse, and this was probably the point we really thought seriously about returning to the UK. Within six months of this family debate, we saw New Zealand's economy start to spiral. A further six months on and New Zealand financiers and politicians finally started to recognize and admit there was an economic problem. Of course Asia and then Russia were blamed for the problems. The government (to my mind) added more to the problems by removing import tariffs, resulting in the slow and sometimes sudden death of any remaining New Zealand businesses.

We had brought funds of $900.000 into the country and were trying to be optimistic, but, as the crisis deepened, the reality could be that four years later we would only take back $400.000 of that. The failing dollar could see a quarter of that lost as we converted it to sterling. On arrival in New Zealand, the exchange rate was 2.4, in September '98 it was 3.3 with every likelihood of sliding further before any improvement! A wonderful exchange rate if taking sterling to New Zealand but devastating the other way around! Throughout the first half of 1999, the exchange rate has hovered around the 3 to 3.1 mark.

Having applied for numerous jobs, we were getting nowhere. The outgoing friendliness of the Kiwis stopped at the point where outsiders were after their few and far between jobs, and who could blame them? At grass-route level, migrants were not welcome. The job descriptions in the newspaper gave us some light relief as we mused over the inflated descriptions and job titles. A shop assistant would become a 'Sales Executive' and some descriptions should have come with a translation from whoever swallowed the dictionary before writing them.

An article in the New Zealand Herald on 16<sup>th</sup> September 1998 further testified to the employment situation, the cause being taken up by an immigrant from Bangladesh who had obviously found the same as us when applying for jobs. He related the 'closed shop' mentality saying, 'There are too many instances of overseas engineers, with all the qualifications and experience sought in a job advertisement... finding themselves never short-listed for interviews.' He had observed how employers, if given a choice, employ a local person. Sadly, whereas we saw it primarily as their 'survival instincts' - he suspected racism as the problem.

Keeping positive was increasingly difficult as we felt gradually destroyed and trapped. The house had been on the market a year, and there was absolutely no sign of work opportunities. John had worked intently on yacht designs for three years with no commissions. He obtained some insurance assessment work, which tended to be seasonal and in short supply but at least enabled him to make some good contacts within the marine industry. At one point, we rented in Auckland with the dual purpose of settling Alistair into his new College, and the hope of work opportunities being greater due to the increased population and higher concentration of marine industries there. Many of the contacts John made, as he relentlessly visited virtually every marine related company in Auckland, will be invaluable, but sadly produced no employment.

We investigated business opportunities with the awful realization that nothing was prospering and most Kiwis scraped by, living very much hand to mouth. If only we had rented instead of built – if only we had got jobs before settling so permanently. How had our dream turned to such despair and when would it end?

In June 1998, the government announced a new initiative to increase migration to New Zealand. Our reaction was horror as we realized what we should have realized before. A country draws on migrants to boost their own economy. An article about the new initiative in the New Zealand Herald June 1998 stated, 'The Minister of Immigration, Max Bradford, last night dismissed a suggestion that the new drive was to address our own economic ills'

You might think so, but I couldn't possibly comment!

Only three months and one new Minister of Immigration later, there was yet another astute article by the New Zealand Herald. On 16th September, under the heading, 'Package to lure 'quality' migrants – big money Asian investors targeted', it pointed out that the target of 38,000 immigrants needed to be increased to 50,000 just to achieve a net gain of 10,000. The previous year had seen a net gain of only 450 due to the large numbers of long-term departures! The article then quoted Mr. Delamere as saying, 'If someone is coming here to invest $1 million or $2 million, the fact that they speak or do not speak English should not matter. If they are businessmen or women they will find their own way around it with interpreters.'

After all why should speaking English matter – money has a language all of it's own! Only months earlier, concerns had been expressed about the number of people unable to speak English, and therefore 'handicapped' in obtaining employment. The other delightful irony or hypocrisy or maybe both, revealed by the article was that Mr. Delamere was a former member of the New Zealand First party, which had in 1996 campaigned to curb immigration.

We were by no means the only migrants suffering. Professionals such as doctors and specialists had tragic stories as well. They had been approved for permanent residency and once there, discovered that they were unable to practice their professions without taking further qualifications, something the New Zealand Government had omitted to tell them. The front page of The New Zealand Herald, September 5th/6th read, 'Migrant misery, our Government owns up'. The article by Andrew Stone, related how an expensive immigration policy blunder had left hundreds of highly skilled settlers facing the prospect of never working in their chosen profession in New Zealand. The Government was drafting a paper that could see some migrants offered 'student loans' to re-enter the workforce in '18 months time'. It also stated that, 'The presence of hundreds of out of work migrants has not deterred the Government from maintaining its 38,000 permanent residency target, with recruitment drives in Hong Kong, Taiwan and Britain'.

Only 15 days later, the Herald struck again with an article entitled, 'Kiwis leaving by plane load, long term exodus stalls overall migration totals.' It stated, 'Faced with a flagging economy, the Minister of Immigration, Tuariki Delamere, has signalled a boost to the immigrant quota from 38.000 to 50.000, but the government has no control over numbers leaving.'

Ironically, an article immediately underneath that one and which had also been run in the Sunday papers, quoted the UK National Opinion Poll research group, as showing that 32% of British adults have seriously considered going overseas to live and of those, 34% would choose Australia and New Zealand as their favourite destination!! I can only hope that 7.31 million read and learn from this book before embarking on that course!

A chance meeting with some British migrants who had moved from Turangi (in the North Island) to Nelson enabled us to hear another sad tale a group of British migrants. These people, like many others, were unable to obtain employment, were living off capital or unemployment benefit and becoming increasingly depressed. We realized how fortunate we were to at least be able to return to England, albeit with depleted finances.

After reading in the newspaper about a Korean couple who had emigrated to New Zealand with their dreams and had now entered a path of despair, our empathy led us to go and visit them. They were trying to run a Korean restaurant, the wife doing all the cooking. The dark circles under her eyes and gentle smile conveyed much. While her husband chatted with us for an hour, she never once sat down. Like many others, they were well educated, he was a Professor of computer science and she was an orthopaedic nurse, with two young children. Unable to practice their Christianity in Korea, they had seen New Zealand as a haven for their children to be brought up in. He related how his children were taunted at school and disbelief broke across his face when we told him our son had been taunted as well, 'But he's white!' he exclaimed. What he had perceived as a racist problem suddenly became an 'immigrant' problem.

The excitement of a favorable exchange rate from sterling to NZ dollars (2.8 at the outset of our plans to emigrate but 2.24 when we eventually took our sterling into NZ) never made us look more closely the other way around. What was it about the other economy this really revealed? Why does a Country suddenly encourage greater immigration? Four years later, trying to sell our property and return to the UK in an increasingly depressed New Zealand economy, we learnt the answers the hard way!

# HELPFUL HINTS!

1. One can only become aware of cultural differences by living in the country.
2. Watch adverts and television programmes to see if they 'irritate' in any way.
3. Carefully consider impact of changing currency back to that of your homeland, should you return.
4. If employment of any kind is needed, make sure it is obtained prior to building or purchasing property.
5. Being aware of all the things mentioned in this chapter can help one to accept them.
6. With sufficient funds and /or employment, it is still a wonderful way of life.
7. Be careful of water supply in certain areas and drink bottled water if in doubt.

# CHAPTER 10

## The real estate minefield

# CHAPTER 10

When we first arrived in Nelson with its population of 40,000, we could not believe the amount of property on the market – let alone the number of Real Estate agents. We still have not really got to the bottom of this and only speculate that there is a fair proportion of properties built by builders on 'speck', and that another proportion is accounted for by people simply raising their standard of living and of course the immigrants building their dream homes! There are eight offices in Nelson city centre alone, all of these having further branches within nine miles and all the agents work on a commission only basis.

We gradually worked our way through most of the local agents in an attempt to sell our property. Generally, we found them to be very friendly but unused to dealing with clients of higher price range properties. The commission only basis did (at the open admission of one agent) lead them to try and sell the house that they would obtain the higher commission on. When I pointed out that, as a client, that approach told me they were not interested in selling me what was right for me, but in what they could get out of it, they quiet unashamedly said, 'yes, that's right'. I suppose they should at least get a point for honesty!

Having a Sales/Marketing background, I would invite a prospective agent around, show them through the property and ask how they would market it. As I had produced a portfolio detailing the whole property (with dimensions) and including seventeen colour photographs that I could make available to them, I felt this was a good fee negotiation point. Agents there really seemed to have little idea of marketing so I also ended up writing most of the copy used to advertise our property. Having a good idea of what else was on the market at that stage and knowing our house had cost a total of $595,000 to build we, believed an asking price of $595,000 to be realistic and necessary. One rather arrogant agent (ruled out of the job) suggested a price of $400,000, he took great offence at my reply when I told him that any idiot could sell anything for less than it was worth and that the real skill in selling is to achieve a higher price!

Selling a property was very different in New Zealand. There were 'Set Sales', tenders, auctions and open homes.

Open homes literally meant opening one's home on a set day and time for people to wander through. Some owners would even provide nibbles for people tramping through. This whole idea was something we were vehemently opposed to as it tended to result in nosy neighbours, and anyone with a free afternoon, arriving to have a good look around. The threat to security, let alone the infringement on one's privacy, ruled this out as far as we were concerned. However, in desperation towards the end we relented on this, *but* only with our version of an 'open home'. It was still publicized in the paper but the door was **not** left open for anyone to wander in. I personally greeted each arrival and was quite happy to dispatch as politely as possible any neighbours. The open home proved to be worse than we anticipated. One couple who the agent had started to show around while I was occupied with another couple, aroused my suspicion. On greeting them, a few polite but direct questions actually revealed them to be agents and not looking to purchase at all. I politely explained this was for perspective purchasers only and showed them to the door. I was furious when I further discovered they had recently amalgamated with the company who organized the open home. If they had had the courtesy to introduce themselves as agents instead of very definitely making out they were perspective purchasers it would have been different. Yet another clear case of un-professionalism, not to mention deception.

It was clear to us from the open home experience that a property like ours in the higher price range would not be sold by an open home. Talking to those we did show around revealed that they were not immediately able to purchase anything.

'Set Sales' is yet another intensive marketing plan, usually over a four-week period, which the 'vendor' pays for. A price range is indicated rather than a set price. To us, this is absurd, if we saw a price range, we would automatically offer the lower price. A large sign with a sailing boat emblem makes it rather corny and is erected outside the property. This is backed up with advertising in the local paper. The alleged origin of the 'Set Sale' is the Australian Americas Cup when house sales boomed, and someone leapt on the phrase to link up with the sailing flavour of the time.

Auctions are generally advertised in a high profile campaign – yes, you've guessed – paid for by the vendor. Again this is often over a four-week period with the auction on a date advertised, which takes place on site. It is unusual for anyone to have a survey in New Zealand, so it would not even be 'subject to survey'. Unless there is a great deal of interest in a property, there really is little point in an auction. The numerous cheap properties can attract several buyers. As in everything else the Kiwis like a bargain.

We had decided to use one agent only alongside our own marketing, 'Joint sole agency with the vendor' is what they called it. Again, by their own admission, the agents told me that if it was a general agency, no one really bothered, so a sole agency was the way to go. Being so far unimpressed by their sales rhetoric, we were cautious to stick to short-term contracts of three months so we could asses if the agent was any use. We were rapidly running through of the abundance of agents – maybe this was why there were so many!

There is only one main newspaper in Nelson and we felt we could cover advertising in this ourselves. We only needed an agent to cover the option of those buyers who walked into their offices to see listings.

Having enlisted an agent, we were advised to run a 'tender' programme. This basically consisted of a four-week intensive marketing programme inviting tenders for the purchase, by a specified closing date. The aim was to flush out any procrastinating purchaser. We would have to pay for the advertising and were told it would cost up to $1000 but that the agent was accountable for the money and we would have a break down of the costs. We decided to do this on agreement that the advertising fees would become payable on sale of the property. The tender date came and went with no interest shown. However, like much of the advertising we paid for, it did generate inquiries for properties of lower prices, which the agent could utilize.

Some months later, we were sent an invoice for $1000. On pointing out our agreement about paying when the property was sold, we didn't have a problem. My request for a breakdown of that $1000 was not replied to until some months later when we had a conditional offer. The breakdown eventually showed a total of $860, **not** $1000 as invoiced. Even within that $860 was a $100 charge for a sign that was never discussed or requested. I had in fact made my own sign, which the agent removed to put theirs in its place.

There was little to choose between the agents, and we stayed with the latest on a 'casual' basis after the expiry of our contract because of the personality of the particular lady we were dealing with. She was a very caring, kind-hearted person who we generally had a good rapport with. Also having worked abroad, she was used to dealing with people of various backgrounds. I increased marketing overseas and was introduced to an agent new to a local company who had great enthusiasm and somewhat more professionalism than most of the agents we had encountered. We decided to let her also handle our house on a casual basis, after her agreeing to our greatly reduced fee due to my supplying marketing material. Once one agent saw the other advertising, it seemed to prod the first into action. The latter of the two was excellent at informing us of the non-events surrounding the marketing, something we did greatly appreciate. It really was vital to keep contact with them otherwise nothing would happen. Our American friends mentioned in a previous chapter had been overseas for three months, leaving their property in agents' hands before going. We had not seen it advertised at all, until one week after their return to New Zealand, out of sight out of mind!

Few prospective purchasers were brought to view our property, and when they did come, I showed them around because I knew I could better explain the many features and present it to its maximum potential. One couple who came seemed to really like the house. After extracting them from the agent who I left with John, due to his unhelpful and unprofessional comments, they opened up more. Finally we left the agent outside and John and I had a more in-depth discussion with the couple, including purchase price and so on. We exchanged telephone numbers as they too commented on the laid-back attitude of the agent! I was mystified and greatly concerned when told by the real estate company that these people were not interested. We then had direct dialogue with them for approximately three months, which resulted in their indicating an offer would be made after a particular weekend. It was a tense wait only to be deflated and incensed by the ridiculous offer they made.

Six weeks later our emotional roller coaster was to soar again. An English couple previously shown around by the agent, we were told, had decided to build. Our concern for what they may go through led us to invite them for coffee. We had been in Auckland at the time they were shown our property and we had never met them. We asked them over, stressing quite earnestly that we were not trying to push our house on them. We had a lovely two hours chatting and warning them of the pitfalls and recommending builders, lawyers and so on. That evening, the phone rang and we were stunned when they told us they had been in turmoil since leaving us and had decided to make an offer on the house. Our increasingly burdened situation led us to accept the offer despite it being $450.000 – far lower than our latest reduced price. This progressed to a conditional two-week contract. Basically on signing, it meant that we were bound by it, but there were various clauses all very loosely worded which enabled them to withdraw if they so decided.

It was an agonizingly long two weeks, at the end of which our worst fears were realized. They phoned and told us they were withdrawing their offer, citing all sorts of building problems. We were devastated, never anticipating any problems with the actual structure of this, high quality, near-new home and immediately contacted the builder who was equally devastated. He in turn contacted the person who had done the report to be told that the report in fact said what a superb house it was. We had the same story fed back to us via the purchasers' solicitor and could only conclude that they were just trying to get out of the contract, which of course they could, with the greatest of ease. It left us emotionally numb, without a buyer and having to put on hold all the preparations we were making to return to England. However, the very next day as is usual for us at times like that, we worshiped and prayed to God. I had an incredible sense that everything would be OK – maybe there was another buyer just around the corner? Half an hour later, the phone rang. The English couple had met with the author of the report and their solicitor and were now declaring they would purchase the house. We were somewhat amazed, as they never even referred to the previous conversation. Our conclusion was that the report, written in an alarmist manner, and read by a reactionary person, had resulted in a disastrous fusion. Two days later, we had a letter via our solicitor saying that they were reducing their offer by a further $15,000. Anger broke through the numbness as we were initially adamant we would not reduce further. Our painful awareness of the economic situation tempered our response, which had been ignited by their strange dealings. An eventual compromise was reached, making the final offer $5.000 less than the first, in reality selling a $595.000 home for $435.000! The shady dealings had not ceased though, our agents would inform us of information they had received via a source from the purchaser's solicitor, the latest of which indicated they were looking at another property. All this played havoc with our emotions. We were yet again appalled by lack of confidentiality, although it was working for us in some respects. Only our faith and trust in a sovereign God kept us sane (at least relatively so) during this period.

We were still waiting for confirmation of the contract becoming unconditional and, as the other party was strangely quiet, I decided to telephone them. The result was that he declared that his integrity had been questioned in a letter from our (genuine, excellent and diplomatic) lawyer and subsequently he had been on the verge of walking away from buying the property. Thankfully, diplomacy took hold of me and it resulted in his declaring the contract would become unconditional that day but it would now be at $430.000! 'Vengeance is mine' says the Lord, and we committed it all to God, trying walk in love and forgiveness towards these people, never having experienced such dealings. Finally the house was sold, although our elation was tempered by the financial loss but – at least the emotional pressure was lifted!

## HELPFUL HINTS!

1. When engaging a Real Estate agent, make sure any contract with them is for a minimum period.
2. Make sure all agreements are in writing.
3. A 'joint agency with the vendor' enables you to sell the property yourself *without* incurring the agents fee.
4. Make sure you have excellent legal advice on all aspects of sale and purchase in New Zealand.

# CHAPTER 11

## Farewell from Auckland

# CHAPTER 11

Someone once said, 'The best laid plans of mice and men...'

As mentioned in the first chapter, patience has never been one of my virtues. Once we had made the decision to leave New Zealand, I was working out dates of return to the UK, itinerary, shipping and all the other necessary details. This is where we started! With nearly four years of stress, we felt we needed a rest and so planned that, when the house was sold, we would spend ten nights in Rarotonga. It would be total relaxation lying in the sun, cycling around the Island, playing tennis and generally uncoiling the springs that had become increasingly taut. Could four years of coiling be uncoiled in ten nights?

Yet another consequence of emigrating are the new holiday destinations one has on the doorstep. The Cook Islands, Fiji, Australia and others were our replacements for places like France, Spain and Greece.

As we progressed towards the sale, despite the roller coaster, I held flights that didn't involve parting with any money. Two to Wellington, where we would collect a hire car and drive to Auckland after visiting the 'Te Papa' museum and friends. A four night stay in Auckland, spending time with Alistair, who by this time was half way through his guitar course and enjoying his new found independence staying in a hostel, would be followed by the Rarotongan holiday. On our return, we would rent an apartment in Auckland for four weeks enabling us to be there for Alistair's graduation. Further flights were being held to the UK, stopping in Vancouver. This departed from Auckland on 4th October. We had decided to stay in Vancouver for a month and somewhere in our discussions we had another thought – what about emigrating to Canada ?! After all, we were hopefully wiser from our experience and knew what we must look for culturally and if we could find work during that one-month stay... and... With these thoughts, we decided to investigate immigration requirements and possibly apply before leaving New Zealand. After all, we did not have to take up the residency if it didn't seem right when there!

Flights were also being held to the UK on Singapore airlines direct to UK except for the fuelling stop. Maybe it would be safer not to let our feet touch ground anywhere else?

Flights and stops were the most enjoyable part to organize although at times I felt as if I was juggling ten things in the air at once. Shipping and packing was the most tedious but, having now moved six times in the last four years, my packing skills were improving greatly. Which clothes did we need for the remainder of our time in New Zealand, which for Rarotonga, which for Canada and which on immediate arrival in the UK? I listed in detail every item in each 'dish pack' - the new word for tea chest!

The low dollar had caught us at every turn and was now also responsible for increased shipping costs. A 40' container door to door was going to cost $16.600, although the exchange rate was then 2.8, it was not relevant as all our money had been converted to NZ dollars. We had an initial quote of $8.900. To cut a long story, very short an unscrupulous employee of a well known shipping company neither put it in writing nor stuck by his word once he had half our belongings in store in Auckland. This resulted in increasing our costs and kicking ourselves for not having had it in writing. Every way we turned, things went wrong and we were reaching the point where we longed to be gone from New Zealand. Within our homeward-bound preparations, we discovered from the shipping agent the number of American, British and other nationalities that he had heard similar stories from and shipped back to their country of origin.

Living in a rental apartment in Auckland had opened another world of experiences. Firstly, I must tell you that the completion of the house sale did progress and the container was duly packed. Our American friends waved us farewell from Nelson airport and we could not help but feel a sadness as the plane took off, remembering only too well our arrival only four years earlier with all our anticipation and dreams. As I tightened my safety belt, I took hold of my emotions – after all, it hadn't worked out there and now we were at least able to move on.

Our brief stay in Wellington went according to plan. Lunching with and saying goodbye to our friends  (Kiwis we had met in England at the launch of 'Enza' and who retired home to Wellington at the time we emigrated) again brought sadness to us. We stayed overnight at The Manor Inn, which we had always used when in Wellington. It had motel style rooms but the room we always booked was on two floors. The upper floor comprising of bedroom with a large spa bath and the lower floor had the kitchen, sitting room and bathroom. The standard of cleanliness and furnishings were excellent, and better still, it had a superb restaurant in the main building with a romantic ambience. On a previous visit we had a very poor quality piece of lamb but the Maitre D', dealt with and rectified the situation so well it really didn't matter.

The drive up to Auckland is a good nine hours and we had decided take it at a leisurely pace and break up the drive by staying overnight in Palmerston North, a slight detour off our normal route but a part we had never seen. We were overwhelmed by the size of the city, having for some unknown reason a preconceived idea that it was small. As we continued on our journey to Auckland, the increased distance from Nelson seemed to ease our emotional wounds and found us looking to the future although we did not know what it would hold. We were at least semi-confident that returning to the UK was a wise decision.

It was wonderful to see Alistair again and before departing to Rarotonga, we left cases we did not need immediately, in his room.

Our night-time arrival of 11pm in Rarotonga found us queuing in a 'stagnant' customs line with a humidity level of 84%. A serenading guitarist keeping spirits light with Pacific Island music and good humour. We entered into conversation with a delightful elderly couple in front of us, so obviously fond and caring of each other and expatriates of the 'old school' - probably more at home on a plantation with servants. It appeared I had now met someone else who did not consider patience to be one of her virtues! Both the wife and I declared we were respectively the most impatient ladies and both our husbands were quick to assert they had the most impatient wife. Finally an agreement was reached on the basis that we both freely admitted lack of that particular virtue. Passports were duly stamped and customs officials seemed relieved to wave us through, only checking more thoroughly a young tanned 'surfy' dragging his cumbersome board in a mid blue cover.

Thoughts turned to 'Tipani Tours', our point of contact so we could be transferred to the hotel. A jovial Rarotongan took our bags and led us to a row of trailers, lifting the lid, he told us we could 'get in'. He appreciated my humour when in reply I asked if it had air conditioning. We decided the bus would be the more suitable option and left the luggage in the trailer. My concern as to whether the bus would connect with the right trailer was misplaced, as the driver manoeuvred onto the trailer with the skill of someone who had done this at least a hundred times before! The bus swayed and jolted along dark roads, which refused to yield any glimpse of Rarotonga. On arrival at the hotel, we were greeted by a very depressed proprietor who told us that his wife was terminally ill and therefore the Restaurant had not been operating for some weeks. Our horror at there being no restaurant was initially overtaken by our compassion for his situation – only later did we feel we had to separate the two situations.

The next morning revealed the first glimpse of where we were. The shower reluctantly yielded water in a steady but weak flow. Ants swarmed around some juice spilt on a table, and ironically, unlike some international hotels, there *was* actually a power point conveniently situated by the mirror, so I could plug in my hair drier and see to style my hair. Looking out of the window revealed a grey day and a roaring ocean crashing on a reef about twenty meters from the white sandy beach. As the surf rolled back down to reunite with the sea, it was an incredible turquoise colour, enhanced by a frame of foaming white.

Our room, an 'Are' with thatched roof and fairly basic, had clean linen and was acceptable despite having had to purchase 'jif' to clean the toilet. We were in the best 'Are' on the property, at the beachfront and with a wooden verandah. The fridge contained a litre of juice and a bottle of sparkling Chardonnay. Our arrival for continental breakfast found us in a wooden structure with a windowless, waist-high surround and a thatched roof. Inside this shelter-type structure were trestle tables covered with grubby checked cloths. Individual cereal packets and a plate of sliced paw-paw, a quarter piece of banana and a slice of orange were served. A jug of juice and basket of toast arrived with a plunger of coffee that tasted suspiciously like boiled water – being coffee addicts, this was quite serious! The structure would have been ideal in good weather but unfortunately it allowed wind and rain to blow right through. Breakfast became an art of trying to eat whilst holding onto tablecloth and serviettes and shield everything from the sandy floor being blown up onto it.

Our intention had been to stay put, totally relaxing, without the restaurant we would have to eat elsewhere. The torrential rain made this practically impossible and our first evening meal consisted of cheese and biscuits (purchased at a local shop during the day) only made more palatable by the sparkling Chardonnay. The next day we decided to investigate alternatives to be transferred to. The Island was easily cycled around in a day and revealed itself to be hardly worth the energy. Rarotonga was clearly a poor country and badly run down. We were told of a terrific restaurant, which we decided to investigate, but it turned out to be a fish and chip shop with tables on the pavement, which accumulated dust as each vehicle drove past. We were tired and disillusioned so decided to at least eat at this roadside diner, but by then our minds were made up, we would return to New Zealand. With the nearest restaurant fifteen minutes walk away, this was not turning out to be the ten nights of 'spring uncoiling' we had intended it to be.

We had been reluctant to tell the proprietor our decision, not wanting to add to his emotional state. He was very understanding though and immediately agreed to refund our accommodation charge in full. Also, he would take us to the airport at 6.30 the next morning so we could take a stand-by flight back to New Zealand. We returned to our 'Are' relieved and packed everything for our early morning departure. At 3am, the fish and chips decided to take their revenge, but I will spare you the detail by merely saying that I had food poisoning! The Air New Zealand cabin staff could not have been more helpful, supplying me with oxygen, cold wet flannels and human kindness. Having flown with numerous airlines, we would say from our experiences that Air New Zealand is one of the best airlines, and the friendliness and efficiency of staff is consistent.

The Nelson branch of this particular travel agent (The Flight Centre) who had been wonderful when making all our travel arrangements (holding numerous flights on various airlines and clearly possessing that virtue of patience which I lacked) had sadly recommended our disastrous hotel and were obviously horrified by our experience. The company dealt with our complaint in the same courteous, friendly and helpful manner in which they had started their dealings with us. We were shocked when, after our return to New Zealand, the proprietor of the Hotel related a completely untrue version of the situation, stating that the restaurant was only closed for two days. We could only put it down to his emotional state and the fact that the agent was possibly trying to recover any refund we were claiming from him. After various telephone conversations and correspondence we settled on a refund figure and although $450 less than the total cost of the holiday, we were satisfied with the way our complaint was dealt with by the Travel agent, which would lead us to recommend them to anyone.

The final four and a half weeks was to be spent in an apartment in Auckland and dealing with rental agents was possibly marginally worse than real estate agents. We did however find two excellent agents amongst them.

When renting an apartment, it is not until one is actually in the apartment that one realizes if it is satisfactory or not. One of our mistakes was to rent a one bedroom apartment with hardly any wardrobe hanging space. I thought I had rectified that problem next time by renting a two bedroom apartment, only to discover that the second bedroom had no wardrobe at all!

Before flying to Rarotonga, we thought we had found a suitable apartment to return to. However, once installed we discovered not only did the oven not work – and in the four days we were there, no one came to fix it – but it was incredibly noisy to the extent I had virtually no sleep in that period. John will sleep through anything! We also discovered 'Road racers'. These are usually young lads who spend the evenings racing and revving their cars around the streets frequently playing explosively loud music at the same time. It appeared that this apartment was in the middle of the circuit these delinquents used and the noise was constant throughout the night. Being in the middle of a grand prix race circuit is definitely not conducive to a good night's sleep, unless of course one has excellent double-glazing, earplugs or a surname such as Hill! This apartment had neither double-glazing nor an oven so we packed and moved yet again.

Prior to leaving the building John went out to buy a newspaper and put our rubbish down the waste chute. He returned very distressed only minutes later – he had inadvertently dropped a letter he was about to post, down the waste chute. Unfortunately he had spent a considerable time laboriously filing in the form to our insurance company in the UK. We eventually found our way via a service lift into the stomach of the machine that had devoured the letter and unceremoniously spat it out into a tall green rubbish bin. A silver chute hovered over the bin making ominous noises, threatening to deposit further waste as we tried to retrieve the letter. Mission accomplished, we found our chariot, the lift, would not respond to our calls for it to extricate us from this final 'waste' land. As I looked at John thinking in Laurel and Hardy style, 'Another fine mess you got me into', we were relieved to see a security button tucked in a corner. On pressing it, a massive gate opened onto a back street leading to the rear entrance of the car park, we burst out laughing at our latest epic adventure! At least we had retained our sense of humour through it all.

The agent, who had only been working for that company for three weeks and clearly felt badly about the situation, told us we had broken the tenancy agreement. We maintained that the landlord had done that by not having the oven working and that people should be warned of the noise. The agent himself was a pleasure to deal with as was the agent who found us the apartment we stayed in until leaving Auckland. However, the rudeness of some agents advertising in the New Zealand Herald was appalling – their abruptness and bad manners left us wondering if they really wanted to do business, and it greatly concerned us that first time visitors would encounter these attitudes.

Having settled happily into our apartment at Quay West, which is one of the best in Auckland, we started to feel civilized again. The apartment block is an 'all suite' hotel with some of the suites or apartments managed privately. The apartment itself was well furnished and consisted of a sitting/dining room, a kitchen with dishwasher, fridge/freezer and of course a working oven, bedroom, bathroom with bath and shower and a separate utility room with washing machine and tumble drier. Wide balconies from the sitting room and bedroom looked across the Harbour Bridge and over the Americas Cup development. Excellent 'hush' glass (a commercial standard thickened glass) prevented unwanted traffic noise. Room service was available through the Hotel side of the apartment block along with a valet service for parking and retrieving our car. One of the porters is called 'James' so I found it amusing phoning the valet service and asking 'James' for the car.

With an indoor pool, gym and sauna, we felt we could enjoy the facilities at the same time as getting fit and finally begin to uncoil.

From the sanctuary of our new base, we started to explore Auckland. Ironically having avoided Auckland during our initial tour four years earlier, we now found ourselves thoroughly enjoying it and had a sense of being 'back in the real world'. The expanse of high rise buildings had been added to most significantly by a piece of architecture that belonged to the future. Looming prominently over the city and clearly visible for miles in every direction, eerily illuminated at night and making one question if aliens had landed in the centre of the city was the 'Sky Tower'.

Driving up Queen Street on our previous visit to Auckland earlier in the year, we were disappointed, thinking that it did not have a decent shopping centre in the city itself. We had found shopping Malls such as New Lynn some 20 minutes away and better quality shops at Newmarket about five minutes away. In reality, there are numerous shops in the city, all off Queen Street and it is fascinating discovering them. I could imagine Fagan sending his 'boys' amongst the intricate streets, pickpocketing as people browse in alley ways and lanes which open onto more lanes, with coffee shops and places too numerous to take in. One could easily take a day to explore each side of Queen Street. There is one very small supermarket in the main street but Newmarket has excellent supermarkets and shops.

The Columbus coffee shop, where fresh ground coffee can be bought or enjoyed on the premises, is a must for any coffee addict. We also discovered 'The Sitting Duck' at Westhaven Marina. A tremendous café with excellent quality and good value food, alcohol, and of course, coffee!

Around the corner from our apartment block, we discovered a store housing various designer names such as Gucci, Dior, Givenchy and others. To our amusement, it also had a 'Harrods' tea room. It gave us a refreshing taste of civilization as we lunched at 'Harrods' and we could almost have thought we were back in England – but for the Kiwi style serving.

Once negotiated, the roads and motorways are really not too daunting, although there is a big oversight in not properly signposting motorway connections, especially travelling North to South. The predominant sign is to Hamilton and as a visitor, you would think you were about to embark on a stretch of motorway that would not release you until reaching Hamilton. However, once on that route it is only a matter of meters before local signs and exit points reveal themselves.

Auckland itself, like most major cities, looks drab and dirty with some sleazy areas definitely to be avoided. Regrettably for some visitors this is the only side they see – something we were painfully aware of whilst attending a yachting seminar in Auckland and meeting up with previous acquaintances from the UK who had been shocked by the visual state of Auckland. Unfortunately, the pedestrian route they took from the hotel to the conference rooms took them through a more run-down part of the city.

There is a great deal of development going on especially with the advent of the Americas cup. Apartments are being built on the waterfront, with some of these being sold from artist impressions and priced from $400,000 to $1.5 million for a three-bedroom apartment. The whole area should look very impressive when completed. With sea and harbour views and the city centre only five minutes walk away, they provide very pleasant city living. Having looked around the show apartments of three of these developments, we found the one with (in our opinion) the worst outside architectural appearance to have the best interior for quality and layout. However, as this was the $1.5 million apartment on show one would expect it to be exceptional. The development with the superior external appearance had very poor interior layout and quality. One of the small, two bedroom apartments had the washing machine and tumble-drier located in a cupboard in the kitchen area. Apartment sizes range from 900sq meters to 1400sq meters approx.

Activity is increasing around the Harbour area as the America's Cup syndicates arrive and start to establish themselves. The Italian syndicate 'Prada' has leased an entire level, as well as the ballroom of one apartment block, for the duration of the America's Cup. It has been stripped and refurbished, decorating it in the Italian colours with ceramic tiles from Italy and incorporating a gym and fitness center.

Auckland is anticipating a boost to the economy from the America's cup and undoubtedly prices on apartments and goods will be increased during that period. There has already been an outcry about excessively high berthing charges being made for visitors to the America's cup. The biggest problem we can visualize, is that of traffic congestion around the City and Harbour-Bridge areas during that period.

During our stay in Auckland, John made many contacts within the Yachting world and became familiar and impressed by the boat-building skills and technology there. We actually delayed our departure on a couple of occasions in the hope that work might materialize. At the same time, we were very aware we were living off capital continually and needed to return to the UK to try and develop business. As a yacht designer of elegant yachts in the traditional style, John could see the opportunities for boats being built in NZ, due to the favorable exchange rate. If work had materialized whilst in Auckland, I think we would have stayed – yes, despite the cultural and economic differences, it is still a beautiful Country where we have some very special, warm hearted Kiwi friends who we miss very much. We made costly mistakes, primarily through lack of knowledge and experience – hopefully this book will help others to get it right!

# HELPFUL HINTS!

1. If renting apartments in Auckland start with the rental agent recommended in the back of the book, we know she is excellent.
2. Larger cities do have their advantages – shopping in Auckland is not to be missed.
3. A Cyber café in the High Street gives access to your e-mail.
4. Short term rentals require advance payment – don't pay more than requested in case there is a problem.
5. Within the City centre most places are within walking distance, this can save a week or more of car rental.
6. A good map of Auckland is essential.

# CHAPTER 12

## Back on English soil –
## Where is the grass greener?

# CHAPTER 12

'...And was the Holy Lamb of God, on England's pleasant pastures seen?' Somewhere from within me, that old hymn had surfaced and with it a stirring passion for being back in England, with it's truly wonderful countryside. In a new way, I felt emotions that must have inspired the lyricist who had written the hymn – yes, this inspirational, noble land had to be where Jesus had walked. There was something solid and dependable that defied explanation. Maybe it was that good old British gene!

With no home to return to in the UK, it was interesting working in reverse. The same facilities were needed on our return to England as we had needed on our arrival in New Zealand. Initially, a furnished rental property until the arrival of our container and then unfurnished. As we would be travelling through Canada for two weeks en route, our first concern was a postal address. We had our respective E-mail addresses, which are a valuable contact point, but we needed post to be forwarded as well. On emigrating, it was incredibly easy to open a post box at the Post Office in Nelson. The post box number was issued and receiving mail prior to our arrival, all simply arranged via fax. The Post Office were quite happy to receive payment on our arrival as logically we could not retrieve the post until they had given us a key.

Trying to make the same arrangement in England was incredibly difficult, despite a friend having posted us a Post Office Services booklet. To hasten the process, I decided to telephone from New Zealand. The telephone numbers, although connecting through to England, gave me a recorded message of, 'This service is not available in your area'. Finally I made contact with an alleged human being in the Post Office and was kept 'on hold' for fifteen minutes whilst he contacted first Oxford and then Southampton branches. Eventually I was told he would fax me the appropriate form immediately. The form was never received and we resorted to phoning England again but this time to a family member who we asked to contact the Post Office on our behalf. It took ten working days to set up the post box, an immediate payment of £42 and a lot of persuasion, as we were not in the Country!

We were beginning to remember and encounter the formalities and procedures of England that we had not experienced during the last, laid-back four years!

The quaint cottage in the New Forest was found, albeit on a temporary basis. A 300-year-old thatched holiday let which we managed to book from New Zealand, having obtained the rental agents fax number from 'Country Life'. The same lessons we had learnt in New Zealand regarding renting in an area prior to taking up permanent residency applied. Having yearned for a quaint thatched cottage prior to our emigration, the realities of living in an old cottage showed us it was not the life for a tall family. Alistair by then a 6'2", 18-year-old seemed to have permanent lumps on his head from colliding with low beams! The lack of natural light from smaller windows caused a gloomy, grubby atmosphere, which was probably added to by the poor cleaning standards of this £320 per week property.

Finding unfurnished rental property proved much harder in England. We were told that it was partly due to the time of year (November). Most holiday lets become a six-month minimum letting over the winter months, so this furnished option was also becoming difficult. We moved from the thatched cottage after two weeks, finding anther holiday let in the New Forest for a further two weeks only. Still living out of suitcases was tiring and tedious – we were beginning to feel very nomadic. The next holiday let was in Chawton, Jane Austin country, in fact right next door to where she had lived. The owners were delightful and had thought out this conversion extremely well, even hand-painting tiles in the kitchen with pictures of actual cottages in the village. An abundant supply of Jane Austin videos kept me content, as we enjoyed the surrounding countryside and continually scoured the papers for unfurnished properties.

We were thankful that our arrival in England was greeted with three days of glorious sunshine, despite being the end of October. To arrive to grey skies (as on our previous return) would have made it that much harder returning. The friendliness of the villagers in Beaulieu also helped enormously and showed us the contrast between the less stressful lives of those living in the country (with time to say hello) as opposed to city dwellers. However, venturing out of the New Forest became a tiring drive and very expensive on petrol. We knew we could not live on an estate, and would have to find a home in the country.

The unfurnished property we eventually found was wonderful and surrounded by fields and trees with wild deer leaping across this enchanting view, which stretched beyond peripheral vision. The first crisp white frost adorning the fields and fencing brought delight to me, yet cries of, 'It's cold' from John. The 200-year old flint cottage, with ceilings over the 6'2" requirement, and additional out buildings for storage was to be our home until – who could say?

As we started to 'live' in sardine country again, those reasons for having emigrated in the first place came back to us. The supermarkets were my worst nightmare. Larger than ever, it took me three hours on one occasion, at what I now find is 'the flag ship' store, and therefore holds every line under the sun. The volume of traffic on the roads is unbelievable and drivers seem to hurtle past at alarming speeds with no regard for wet weather conditions. The beauty of the countryside is, to me, as spectacular as the scenery in New Zealand, just in a different way. I had missed the bluebell woods, neatly fenced farmlands, glorious autumnal colours and quaint historic villages.

The price of properties both for sale and rental is horrific. Our flint, three bedroom unfurnished cottage, with only one bathroom, was costing us £1005 per month, the equivalent in New Zealand but with a swimming pool, cost us $840 per month (£350 per month). Generally, we had found the cost of living, without any mortgage or rent, to be around $3000 per month (£1250). That included rates, food and household goods, electricity, insurance (household, car and medical) and running a car. However, the cost of living is always relative to earnings wherever you go. So, once living in New Zealand, if earning Kiwi wages, it is no longer a lower cost of living. If arriving in New Zealand with sufficient funds for the rest of your life and no necessity to work, then it is a lower cost of living.

There had been many times in New Zealand that I had wished I could pop into Marks and Spencer – it had become a joke with my Kiwi friends. I believe it was a mixture of remembering things in a more favourable, exaggerated way, and what I see as the reasons for Marks and Spencer declining profits, that led to my disappointment. The general sales staff did not have the same friendly and helpful attitude, which had set them apart from some of their counterparts in the retail industry in years gone by. As an ex Departmental Supervisor for Marks and Spencer (from 1976-1979) I was appalled by the marked decline in the sales floor staff's attitude. However, a complaint with a faulty product was dealt with extremely well by the Manageress. The previous high precision of departmental and goods layout had disappeared, even during 'sale' periods, goods would have been displayed to maximum effect. Now racks only ever used for transporting goods from the stockroom to the sales floor were lined up in an unsightly, down-market, bargain basement fashion, not worthy of what had once been the crème de la crème in retail. Within the food sector? - Well, I think I had been re-educated by the Kiwis and had become more industrious, creating more of my own gastronomic delights, which I knew were not genetically modified! We also found our palate had changed and the ready-made desserts and tarts were far too sweet and sickly. Having missed these delicacies for four years, it was rather ironic to say the least.

Reuniting with family had to be the best part of returning. We did also remark on several occasions how wonderful it was to be able to converse with people on a deeper, more educated level. Conversely, whereas in New Zealand at times we had found it over familiar to be called by our Christian names, we now found ourselves preferring in certain situations that people should call us by our Christian names! What fickle creatures we are.

Settling back to life in England was proving harder than we realized – letters from friends in New Zealand would initially see me burst into tears. I'd long to have a coffee and chat with them – people who didn't have the pompous barriers that we British tend so often to erect in relationships, as our etiquette often rules our hearts.

As rain and bitter cold winds set in, we found ourselves asking what on earth we were doing back in England? Then of course we would remind ourselves of the serious economical situation there and that we could not find work or develop John's yacht designs with such a small population – and the even smaller population of those that could even afford to build a yacht of £1 million plus.

Discussing everything, we decided that the cultural differences were only important in as much as one needs to be aware of the differences in order to adjust and integrate properly. We felt if we returned, those things would no longer bother us and we would have a less 'British' attitude. There would still be a lack of venues such as theatre and antique fairs, but one could fish and enjoy an all-year-round, outdoor way of life. Knowledge, and subsequent acceptance, also overcomes the difference in substantiality, relating to the way houses are built.

False expectations are the biggest obstacle for migrants. We would earnestly not have considered ourselves to have had any preconceived ideas, but subconsciously, we obviously did have.

Surely the grass is always greener on the other side!

We reminded ourselves of some elderly acquaintances, who have just returned to England from New Zealand, for the fourth time – is there, a deeper spiritual problem? I had mused at one time that New Zealand reminded me of how the ships in ancient mythology would be lured by the beauty of the Sirens, only to be trapped and loose their lives!

The debate ensues and the ideal for us would be to be able to spend eight months in England and four in New Zealand. That has to signify that our hearts are in England, except of course in winter! Six months after our return, the traffic is less daunting as we again become accustomed to it. Return to New Zealand could only be possible by finding an existing, or establishing, an economically viable business. As our respective businesses begin to develop in England, we look forward to staying, but occasionally visiting our 'adopted homeland'.

Our lack of knowledge over building a house cost us nearly £69,000, the declining NZ$ would cost us a further £28,000, totalling £97,000. If this book can save anyone else the loss of nearly £100,000, it has to be an excellent investment for under £11.

# HELPFUL HINTS!

1. Be totally aware there are social and cultural differences.
2. Make sure employment is gained and pays sufficiently.
3. If you emigrate and decide to return, initially visit your homeland. Leaving belongings in storage is ultimately cheaper than shipping backwards and forwards.
4. Only take finances immediately necessary – just in case.
5. Do not be lured simply by beauty – at the end of the day one needs more than aesthetics and climate.
6. Plan to live there for a year before making any decisions.
7. Think extra carefully about everything you are leaving in your Country of origin.
8. Be aware that you will be very unsettled if you emigrate and return, but don't let that make you rush back again.

## FINAL WORD

I sincerely hope this book will be of great help to many with plans and dreams of emigrating. Dreams are wonderful things, which need care to fulfil without incurring disillusionment.

Please feel free to contact me at the addresses below, if I can be of any help in your plans to emigrate.

E-mail:            <u>Livingwords@hotmail.com</u>

Web site:        http//www.livingwords.net

Postal Address:  PO Box 36
                 Dartmouth
                 TQ6 9YP

# USEFUL CONTACT NUMBERS

please note only specific services we have personally used and been impressed by are listed, with the exception of Schools and Colleges.

## AIR LINE
Air New Zealand
UK, London
Tel:   0181 741 2299

## ARCHITECTS
Nelson:
Ian Jack and Associates; 23 Shelbourne Street, Nelson
Tel:   0064 3 548 1372
An award winning architect, professional and although expensive, cost effective at the end of the day

## BANKS
Auckland:
Head Office ASB BANK Migrant Division Queen Street, Auckland
Tel:   0064 9 302 1988  fax: 0064 9 307 2930
E-mail asbmigrant@asbbank.co.nz
Exceptionally helpful and efficient bank
London:
Commonwealth Bank of Australia, Senator House, 85 Queen Victoria Street, London EC4V 4HAP
Tel:   0170 710 3990  fax: 0171 7103939

## BOOK SHOP
Nelson:
Scripture Union, Montgomery Square Car Park, Nelson
Tel & Fax: 0064 3 5483387

## BOOKSHOPS contd.

Wellington:
Pinnacle Books  142 Wills Street, Wellington
Tel:   0800 888 004
Freephone from within New Zealand, excellent, efficient mail order book service as well as shop.

## BUILDERS AND RELATED SUPPLIES

Nelson and Marlborough region:
Ross Lovell, Foley Road, RD 1 Upper Moutere, Nelson
Tel:   0064 3 540 2684
-Excellent builder, usually booked months ahead
Dave Webber
Tel:   mobile: 025 356979
-Conscientious, very helpful and excellent builder
QUANTUM
New Zealand
Tel:   0064 3 540 3204
Hot water system as detailed in chapter 7
Quantum International, Australia
Tel:   61 2 9282 6911  fax: 61 2 9281 0797

## CAR RENTAL

Maui Camper Vans 36 Richard Pearce Drive, Mangere, Auckland
Tel:   0064 9 275 3529  fax: 0064 9 275 9019
E-mail: nzinfo@maui-rentals.com
Budget Car Rental 83 Beach Road Private Bag 92144 Auckland
Tel:   0064 9 375 2220  fax: 0064 9 375 2221

## FERRY SERVICES

Inter-Islander
Tel:   0800 802 802
From Picton in South Island to Wellington in the North Island and back, takes approx. 3 hours each way.

## FERRY SERVICES contd.

The Lynx

Tel:   0800 802 802

From Picton in the South Island to Wellington in the North Island and back, a 74- metre Catamaran taking approx. 1½ hours each way.


## HOTELS

Auckland:        Copthorne, Anzac Avenue

Tel:   0064 9 379 8509

A good mid priced Hotel with excellent service and walking distance to downtown  Auckland

Auckland:        Quay West All Suite Hotel, 8 Albert Street, Auckland

Tel:   0064 9 309 6000  fax: 0064 9 309 6150

Excellent top quality serviced apartments with pool/sauna and gymnasium- see also under Rental Agents (Sandy Evans)

Christchurch:  Commodore Airport Hotel, 447 Memorial Avenue, Christchurch

Tel:   0064 3 358 8129  fax: 0064 3 3582231

Superb mid priced hotel with pool and gym excellent food and service. Driving distance approx. five mins to airport and ten to City centre.

Nelson:        The Quality Hotel, Trafalgar Square, Nelson

Tel:   0064 3 546 3000  fax: 0064 3 546 3003

Recently refurbished higher priced but excellent value and quality, good central location for Nelson City.


## GENERAL INSURANCE

New Zealand Insurance  105 Trafalgar street, Nelson

Tel:   0064 3 548 2119  fax: 0064 3 546 9440

## IMMIGRATION
UK, London:
New Zealand House, 80 Haymarket, London, SW1Y 4TNQ
Tel:   0171 93084 22

## LAWYERS
Nelson:
Pitt and Moore (contact Graham Allan) 78 Selwyn Place, Nelson
Tel:   0064 3 548 8349  fax: 0064 3 546 9153
-A real gentleman and switched on lawyer, very professional practice

## MEDICAL INSURANCE
Southern Cross Healthcare: 181 Graffton Road, Auckland
Tel:   0064 9 356 0911  fax: 0064 9 356 0930

## MOTELS
Nelson:
Riverlodge Motel    31 Collingwood Street, Nelson
Tel:   0064 3 548 3094
Wellington:
The Manor Inn, Cnr Ngauranga Gorge and Newlands Rd., Johnsonville.
Tel:   0064 4 4787812  fax: 0064 4 478 1342
Taupo:
Boulevard Waters Motor Lodge, 215 Lake Terrace Taupo
Tel:   0064 7 377 3395  fax: 00643 7 377 2241

## NEWSPAPERS
UK:
New Zealand Outlook, Consyl Publishing and Publicity Ltd., 3 Buckhurst Rd., Bexhill-on-Sea Sussex
Tel:   01424 223111

## NEWSPAPERS contd.

Auckland:
The New Zealand Herald, 46 Albert Street, Auckland
Tel:    0064 9 379 5050  fax: 0064 9 373 6421
Christchurch:
The Press   Cathedral Square, Private Bag 4722 Christchurch
Tel:    0064 3 3790940  fax: 0064 3 3648498
Nelson:
Nelson Evening Mail,  15 Bridge Street, Nelson
Tel:    0064 3 548 7079  fax: 0064 3 5469462
Wellington:
The Dominion   PO Box 1297 Wellington
Tel:    0064 4 474000  fax: 0064 4 474058

## PHYSIOTHERAPISTS

Nelson:
Sports and Spinal Physiotherapy (Nelson) Ltd. 63 Collingwood
Street, Nelson
Tel:    0064 3 548 8580
- A first class physio who really thinks out a problem, cares, gets re-
sults and has a terrific sense of humour, contact Sheryl Bier or Mike
Munt.

# POST OFFICES

Nelson:
New Zealand Post Ltd., 86 Trafalgar Street, Nelson
Tel:    0064 3 546 7818
Auckland:
New Zealand Post Office Ltd. 69 Shortland Street, Auckland
Tel:    0064 9 307 0661  fax: 0064 9 366 6097

## QUALIFICATIONS AUTHORITY

UK, Cheltenham:
NARIC
Tel:    01242 260010    fax: 01242258611

## QUALIFICATIONS AUTHORITY contd.
New Zealand, Wellington
NZ Qualification Authority
Tel:    0064 4 802 3000

## REAL ESTATE
Nelson:
Wadsworth and Dick First National (Frances Gilbertson)
Tel:    00643 540 2697  fax: 00643 544 7198
NZ Real Estate: Webb site: http://www.realenz.co.nz

## RENTAL AGENTS
Auckland:
Sandy Evans Realty, PO Box 74237, Market Road, Auckland.
Tel:    0064 9 630 4322  fax: 0064 9 630 6758
Email:  sandy@sandy-evans-realty.co.nz
Contact Sandy Evans- totally professional and helpful with some ex-
cellent apartments.
Serviced Apartments Ltd., PO Box 46-252, Herne Bay
Tel & Fax:                0064 9 376 6744
Not used personally, but did stay at one of the mid range apartments
contact Kiven Riley he manages

## RESTAURANTS
Auckland:
The Sitting Duck Café,  141-151 Westhaven drive Westhaven
Marina
Tel:    0064 9 376 0374
Nelson:
Jacaranda Park Garden Café  College Street, Motueka
Tel:    0064 3 528 777  fax:  0064 3 528 7797
Dramatic views of Motueka Valley stretching for miles. Excellent
presentation of food, good value and quality.
Pomeroy's Café and Wine Bar  276 Trafalgar Street, Nelson
Tel:    0064 3 548 7524
A favourite spot for just coffee, cakes, light snacks or main meals,
excellent in every way.

## RESTAURANTS contd.

The Honest Lawyer Country Pub 1 Point Road, Monaco, Nelson

Tel: 0064 3 547 4070 fax: 0064 3 547 4170

Worth finding a traditional English style pub in lovely setting on waterside, good extensive menu snacks and main meals (can't make a proper Cornish pasty- despite the Landlord originating from Cornwall!) Also have accommodation.

The Walnut Restaurant and Bar 251 Queen Street, Richmond

Tel: 0064 3 544 6187

The best restaurant we found for a more gourmet meal and we tried most of them! Only open in evenings.

## SCHOOLS AND COLLEGES

Auckland:

Excel School of Performing Arts

Tel: 0064 9 8277327 fax: 0064 9 8277328

Diverse courses majoring in, guitar, dance, drama or vocals, first year by audition, second year by selection

Christchurch:

Christ's College Rolloson Avenue, Private Bag 4900, Christchurch

Tel: 0064 3 366 8705 fax: 0064 3 364 5295

Private school with boarding facility and excellent reputation.

Nelson College for Boys Waimea Road, Nelson:Nelson

Tel: 0064 3 548 3099 fax: 0064 3 546 6932

Has boarding department, school for boys aged 13-18 years.

Nelson College for Girls Trafalgar Street South, Nelson

Tel: 0064 3 548 3104 fax: 0064 3 546 7251

Has boarding department, school for girls aged 13-18 years.

Waimea College Salisbury Road, Nelson

Tel: 0064 3 544 6099 fax: 0064 3 544 1052

Co-ed for 13-18 year olds.

Nayland College 166 Nayland Road, Nelson

Tel: 0064 3 547 9769

Co-ed for 13-18 year olds.

**TRAVEL AGENT**
Nelson:
The Flight Centre, 199 Trafalgar Street, Nelson
Tel:    0064 3 546 8378
Other branches throughout New Zealand, our contact Dianne Rossier who was incredibly helpful but impressed by other staff in that branch as well.

# MAP SHOWING MAIN CITIES IN NEW ZEALAND

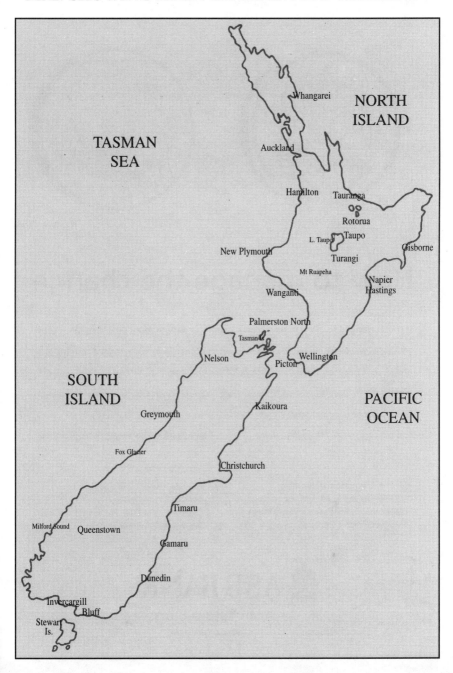

# How to manage the change

If you've decided to move to New Zealand, having a bank account up and running when you arrive will make everything else run a lot smoother. Before leaving the country, plan ahead, and open an account with ASB BANK. You'll be joining one of New Zealand's longest established banks, with an unrivalled reputation for technological innovation and a level of personal service that you'll warm to.

Call today on 0171 710 3990 to get your copy of an ASB BANK Migrant Banking package.

**ASB BANK Representative Office**
c/o Commonwealth Bank of Australia
Senator House, 85 Queen Victoria Street
London EC4V 4HA

**ASB BANK Migrant Division**
Auckland, New Zealand
Ph: (+64 9) 302 1988, Fax: (+64 9) 307 2930
asbmigrant@asbbank.co.nz

## ASB BANK
### Your future bank.
www.asbbank.co.nz

ASK.280.TBWA